AF576546

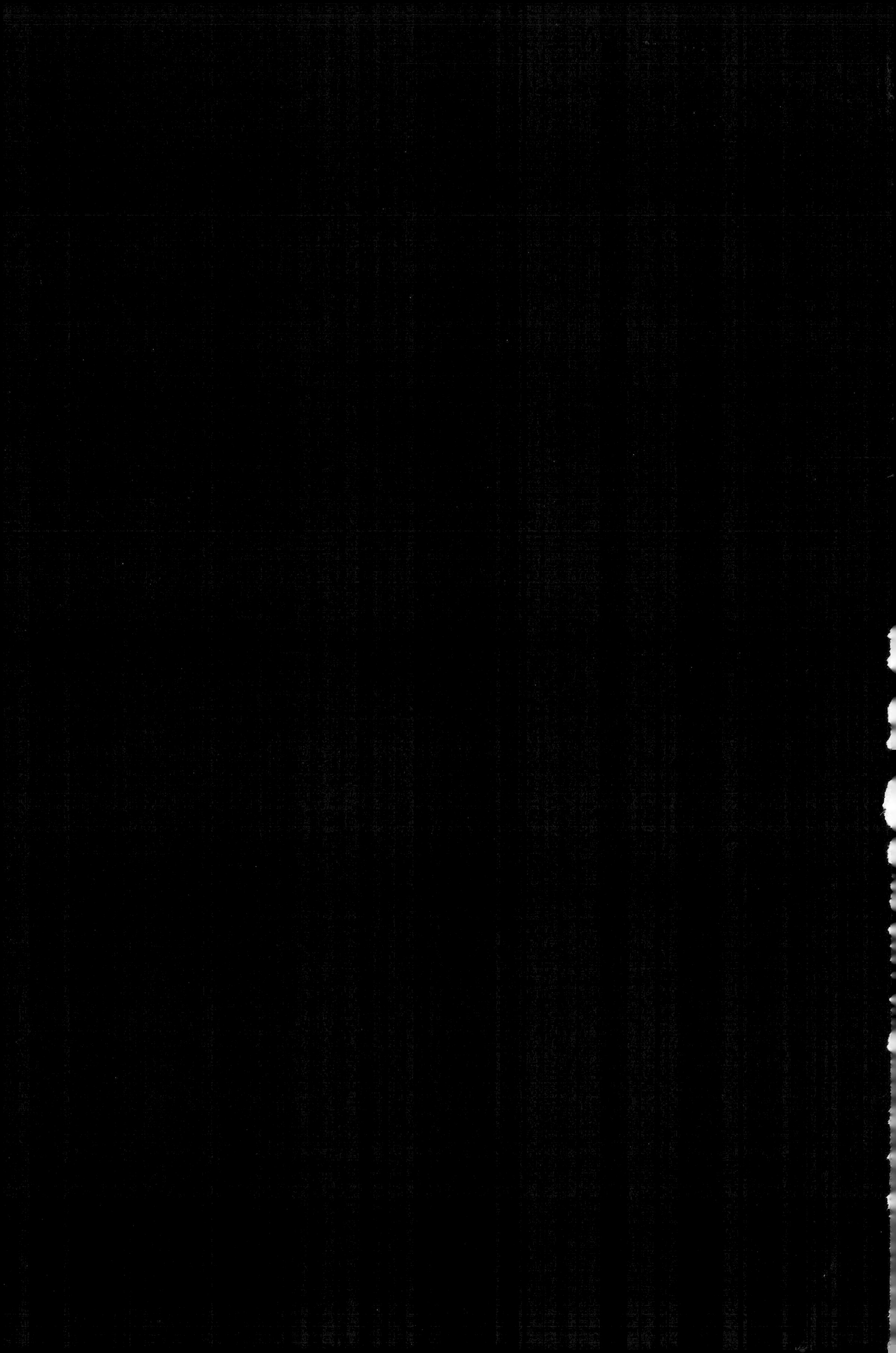

Marc Leuthold

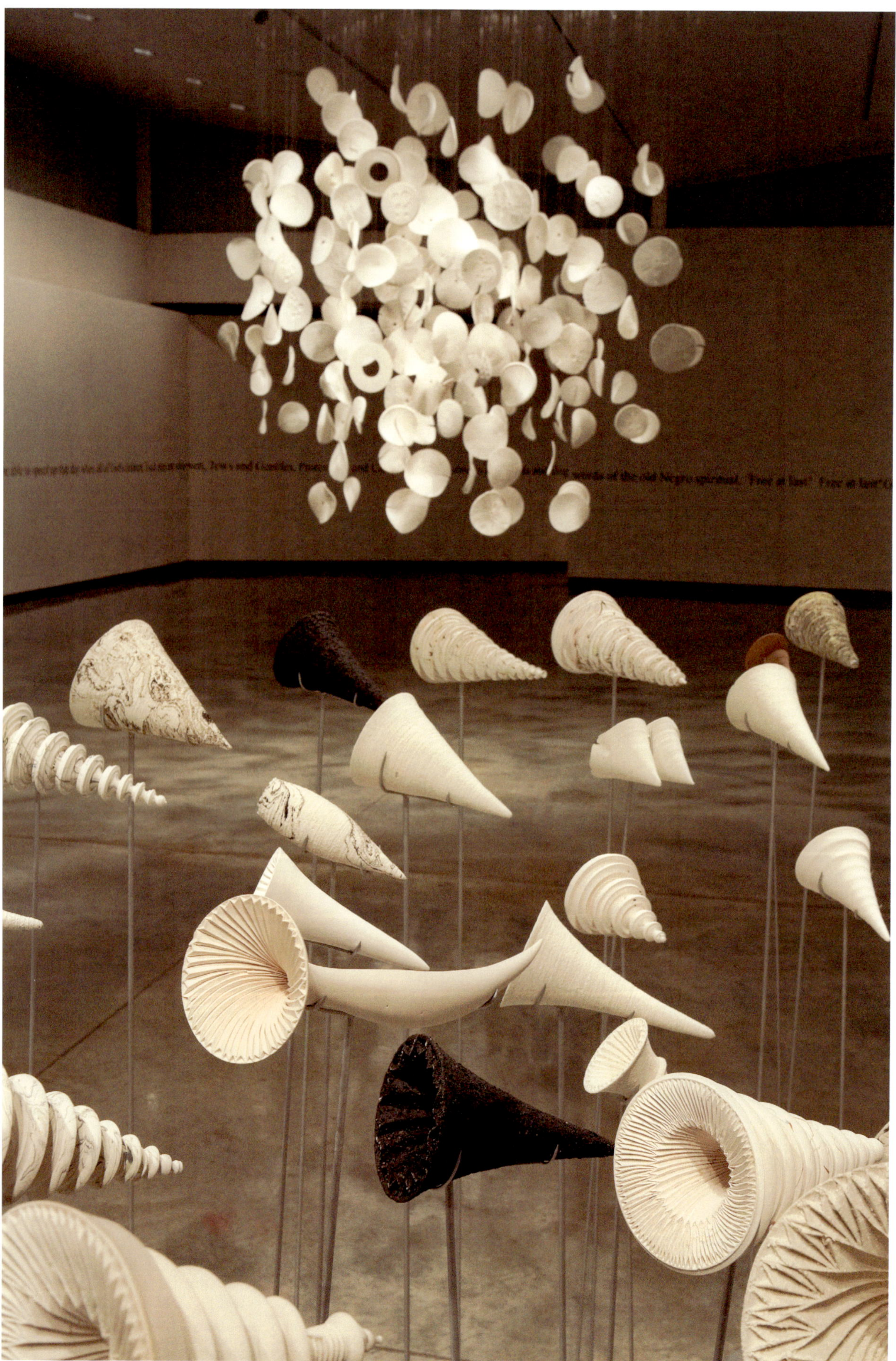
words of the old Negro spiritual, "Free at last! Free at last!"

Marc Leuthold, Sculpture, 1995-2010

Organized by Thomas Piché Jr.
with essays by Phong Bui and Tanya Hartman

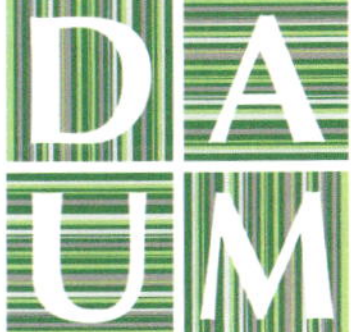

This volume was published in conjunction with the exhibition *Marc Leuthold, Sculpture, 1995-2010* held at Daum Museum of Contemporary Art from February 5 until August 1, 2010, organized by Thomas Piché Jr.

Major funding for this exhibition was received from the Windgate Charitable Foundation. Additional funding came from the Missouri Arts Council, a state agency. Further assistance was provided by Ditzfeld Transfer, Inc.; The State University of New York at Potsdam; Fondation Bruckner, Geneva, Switzerland; and Lehmhuus AG, Basel, Switzerland. All programs at the museum are supported by State Fair Community College and the members of Daum Museum of Contemporary Art.

Daum Museum of Contemporary Art
State Fair Community College
3201West 16th Street
Sedalia, Missouri 65301-2199
T 660-530-5888
F 660-530-5890
www.daummuseum.org
info@daummuseum.org

Museum Director: Thomas Piché Jr.
Museum Specialist: Marcie Teter
Museum Coordinator: Victoria Weaver
Production and Design: Cheryl Landers,
SFCC Marketing and Communications

Printing: Harvest Graphics

PRINTED IN USA

Photography credits—Eva Heyd: front and back covers, pp. 39, 40, 41, 43, 46, 47, 49, 51, 52, 53, 55, 56, 57, 59, 60, 61, 63, 64, 65, 66, 68, 69, 70; Kevin Sisemore: pp. 2, 8, 14, 19-20, 24, 29; Marc Leuthold: pp. 21-22, 25, 27, 28, 30-31, 32, 33, 34, 35, 36, 44-45.

Library of Congress Control Number: 2011937294
ISBN# 978-0-9822507-4-7

Front cover: *Pagodas*, 2010, porcelain.
Back cover: *Keskemet Pagoda*, 2010, marbleized porcelain.
Frontispiece: Installation view of *Offering*, Daum Museum of Contemporary Art, February 2010.

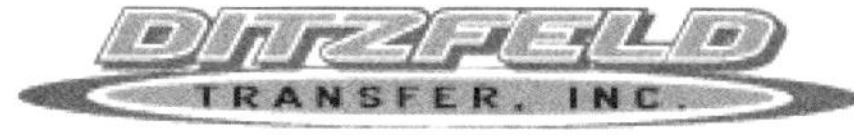

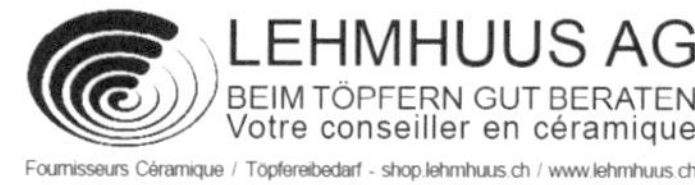

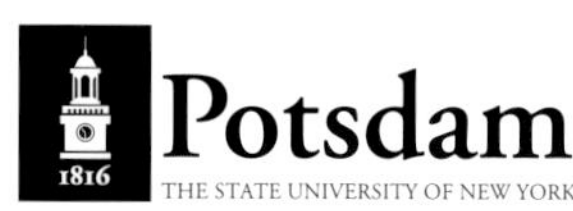

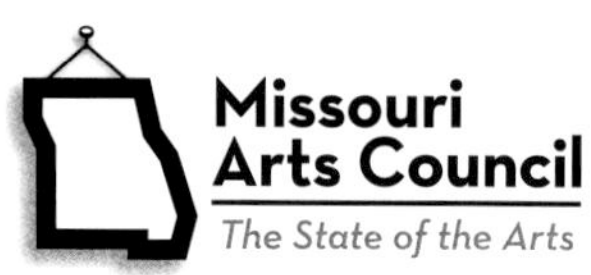

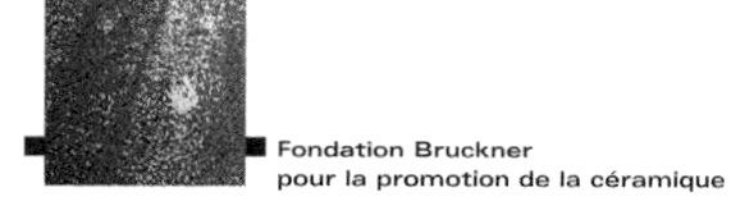

Introduction and Acknowledgments

Like many people, I have long considered Marc Leuthold one of the leading ceramists of his generation. Since the early 1990s, the art world has watched Leuthold's praxis evolve from the display of discrete, intricately carved ceramic discs, wheels, and hemispheres to more ambitious congregations of objects, often assembled in support of ideological premises. This panoply of objects reveals a consistency of artisanal ability and a conceptual congruity, unique to him, that are equally compelling for the viewer. He is, today, highly regarded for the formal and procedural complexity of his work and praised for his ability to evoke spiritual, metaphysical, or cosmic affinities through the display of sculpture that is essentially nonfigurative.

I first became acquainted with Leuthold and his work in 1993, while I was curator at Everson Museum of Art in Syracuse, New York. Leuthold was included in the Everson's 29th *Ceramic National*, and his earthenware sculpture *Red Shard* was one of its highlights (and subsequently became part of the permanent collection of the Mint Museum of Art in Charlotte). Since that time, we have visited in his studio on many occasions, collaborated on ceramics exhibitions (including his first solo museum show), and journeyed together to ceramics events in the United States and abroad. The organization and presentation of this particular retrospective was on my mind even before I first began the directorship of the Daum in early 2008. Our long association makes its realization an especially welcome occasion.

Marc Leuthold, Sculpture, 1995-2010 offers a retrospective look at the full range of work that the artist has produced during the past fifteen years. Included are examples of his signature sculptural forms as well as more recent assemblies of ceramic cones, stacks, dyads, and receptors. The central feature of the exhibition, however, is the premiere of a large-scale environment created by Leuthold specifically for his showing at the Daum Museum. Entitled *Offering*, the installation reveals a mature juncture in the artist's œuvre, where his diverse sculptural tropes are evocatively grouped, matched to an appropriated text, and purposefully staged in correlation with a lambent gallery space. This convincing mix of genres, considered as a single work of art, challenges viewers to synthesize aesthetic presence, poetic allusion, and historic reference.

The essays and illustrations contained in this catalogue illuminate Leuthold's significant accomplishments and provide useful points of entry into his art practice. The inclusion of his statement concerning the installation *Offering*, which details the particular historical events that inspired its production, will lead viewers to a more layered consideration of it. Phong Bui, in his knowledgeable essay, points to Leuthold's place in the broad context of world art as well as in a more specific philosophical lineage. Tanya Hartman, in her well-reasoned review of *Offering*, seizes on its specific backstory and teases out the narrative potential of the work, claiming for Leuthold an engaged role, one that is more concerned with the social and political than the spiritual, metaphysical, or cosmic. I am thankful to both our essayists for their willingness to contribute these helpful statements.

The presentation of *Marc Leuthold, Sculpture, 1995-2010* at the Daum Museum marks an important milestone for us. For the first time, the museum played a critical role in the creation of a major new work of art, *Offering*. By securing funding from a group of benefactors, the Daum was able to afford the artist the ways and means to realize his ambitious project. Leuthold spent three months during the summer of 2009 working on *Offering* at Les Ateliers Céramiques de la Fondation Bruckner in Geneva, Switzerland. There he enlisted the expertise of two studio assistants, Charlyne Kolly and Samuel Gäumann, and together they went into production to create many of the hundreds of porcelain discs and cones that make up the installation.

The Daum is deeply indebted to this ad hoc consortium of patrons. Chief among them is the Windgate Charitable Foundation, an organization that has a stellar record of providing significant support to artists and art institutions involved with craft media. The Missouri Arts Council, a state agency, also provided critical funding for the project. Ditzfeld Transfer, Inc., played an important role in the transportation of objects to the museum. Additional assistance for the project was received from Fondation Bruckner, Geneva, Switzerland; and Lehmhuus AG, Basel, Switzerland.

Consortium funding also allowed staff at the Daum to team with Darrell Jones, who designed and fabricated the complicated mounting system for the installation's two groupings of cones, and to secure the seasoned expertise of Alan Weaver. The installation greatly benefited from their knowledgeable participation as well as that of State Fair Community College art instructor Don Luper. Thanks to each of them for their invaluable assistance.

Gratitude also extends to my colleagues at the Daum Museum: Vicki Weaver, Renee Weller, and, later, Marcie Teter contributed their multifaceted talents unstintingly and effectively throughout the course of the exhibition. Thanks also to Cheryl Landers who devised an especially sympathetic design for the exhibition catalogue and oversaw its production with unflagging good spirits. Appreciation goes to SFCC interns Dustin Mothersbaugh and Lexi Holloway, who helped in a variety of meaningful ways.

Finally, I must express to Marc Leuthold the museum's gratitude, as well as my own thanks, for his creative, unselfish, and patient collaboration on this project. From the initial conceptual sketches to the placement of the final pagoda, Marc's enthusiastic participation has been critical to the successful mounting of this retrospective. Everyone who experiences *Offering* is indebted to the artist; although the catalogue documents only the shadow of its fascination, for now that must be enough.

Thomas Piché Jr.
Director

Offering

This installation incorporates many cone forms inspired by the Nara Period of eighth century Japan. At that time, Japan was going through a difficult period. In A.D. 764, as an act of atonement, Empress Shotoku commissioned one million wooden, conically shaped pagoda forms, each containing a scroll of Buddhist scripture called the *Daranikyo* sutra (*Dharani*). Ten temples each housed 100,000 of the pagoda forms. It was believed that this gesture would help a worried people get through bad times. The eighth century cones were mostly identical, and some of my more elaborate cones resemble the antique ones.

I did not feel compelled to make a million of them, nor was I seeking to duplicate those from the Nara period. The eighth century cones were wooden and mine are made of many different types of clay. The variety of shapes, colors, and textures, both coarse and refined, creates a diverse group, a population. Two groups of about eighty cones each greet the viewer entering the large Douglass Freed Gallery at the Daum Museum. They are mounted on metal bases that range in height from twenty-four to fifty inches. The cones are presented horizontally, tilted slightly upward, so that the viewer can see the carved interiors.

Further back into the space, near the center of the room, hangs a cluster of porcelain discs and shards, roughly 160 pieces. The discs, inspired by *bi* discs from Neolithic China, range in diameter from seven to eleven inches and form a roughly spherical cloud. Buried with the dead, the ancient Chinese discs are circular with a hole in the middle. The circle was a symbol of the universe, and the hole in the middle was believed to allow the soul of the deceased to pass through and to ascend to the heavens. The suspended cloud of gently turning discs appears to hover behind the two circular groupings of cones.

On the three walls of this large room is an excerpt from Coretta Scott King's autobiography, *My Life with Martin Luther King, Jr.* In this text, Mrs. King quotes from Dr. King's "I have a dream" speech and describes the reaction of his deeply moved audience. Like the effect noted on the original audience, the Kings' words send shivers through me today and evoke strong emotions. In this installation, Mrs. King's words define the space and encircle and cradle the cones and the cloud of discs. They guide viewers to search for the meaning of the exhibit, and its more discreet political dimension.

In Coretta Scott King's book, she describes in detail her family's struggle to earn dignity and respect for all Americans, detailing how the government was actively suppressing and oppressing the people. MLK and the Southern Christian Leadership Conference devised ways to fight and correct the system. The struggle was daunting but, through heroic determination, wisdom, and faith, people stuck together and fought against fear and unimaginable injustices. I find this deeply inspiring and relevant to our problems today.

I see ours as a singular moment in the history of the Republic. Suddenly, after years of what I view as bankrupt leadership, we have managed to place in power someone who, I dearly hope, is a man for the people, someone who, like the Kings, can help us face today's challenges. (This was written in June 2009.) But can he right our ship of state, or is the damage of the last forty years irreparable? Do even good leaders become part of a dark system that has gradually weakened our country? What can we do to help ourselves? When does it become our duty to take back our government? My *Offering* is an attempt to call attention to these questions and to the need for all of us to work together to solve our urgent national problems. All that America stands for is at stake.

Marc Leuthold
February 2010

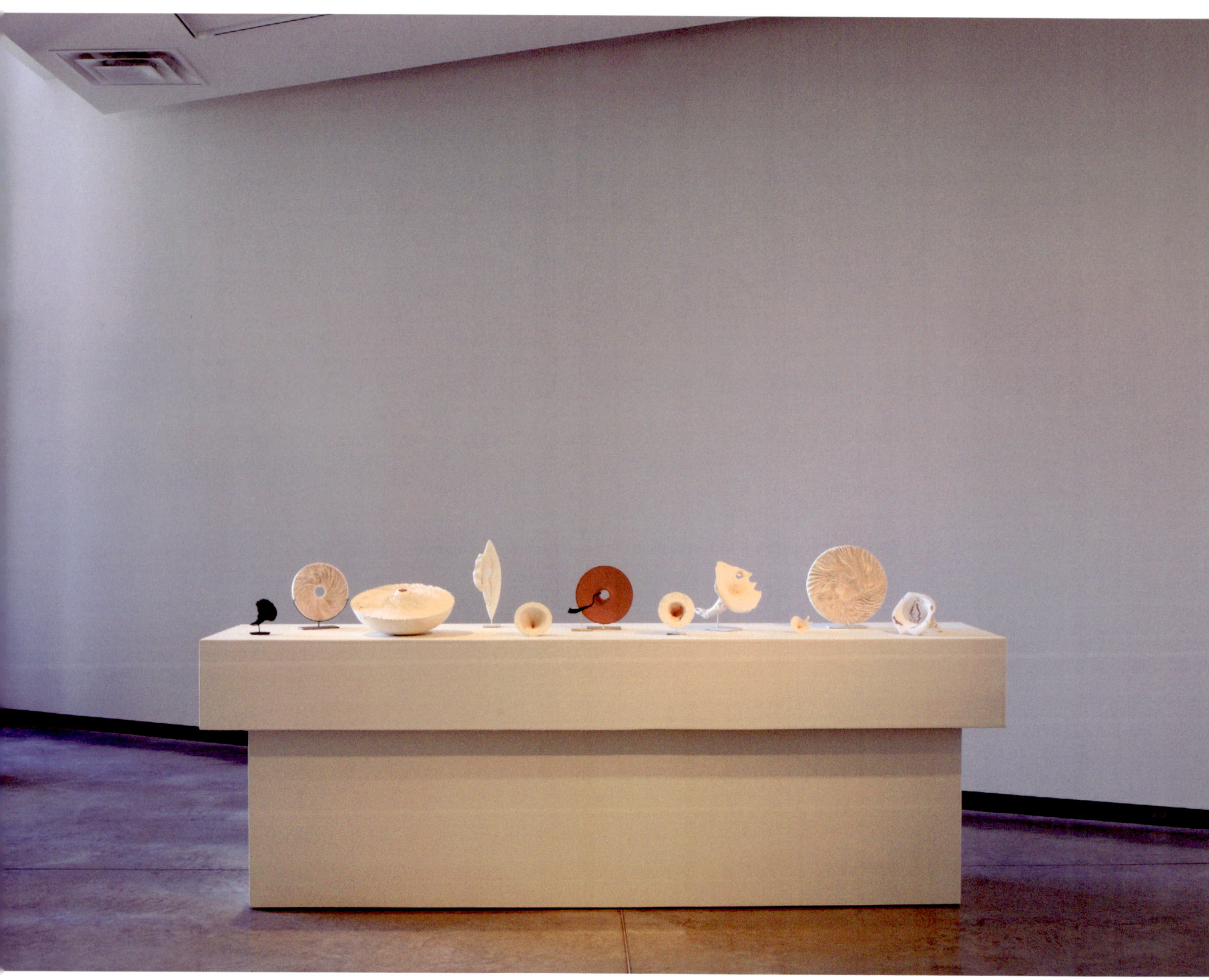

Phong's Table, on view in the exhibition *Marc Leuthold, Sculpture, 1995-2010,* at Daum Museum of Contemporary Art, February 2010.

Marc Leuthold: An Offering to All

One of the most striking features of Marc Leuthold's legacy is that he has managed to carve out a unique space within a set of boundaries that has redefined how ceramic as a medium and the artists who work with it are perceived.

With the exception of Picasso, who single-handedly catapulted ceramic art to prominence in the late 1940s, and the generation of artists whose work is associated with the California Clay Movement of the 1950s (Peter Voulkos, Ken Price, Billy Al Bengston, Betty Woodman, Andrea Gill, and others) who generated various pictorial possibilities springing from abstract expressionist aesthetica, surrealist fetishization, assemblage, funk sculpture, pop image, and other decorative tendencies that adhere to the interplay between patterning and illusionary depth and volume, there has been increasingly less of the collective effort to support any kind of network among artists who work in this medium.

Yet, from the East Coast perspective, particularly in the last two decades, there have been few artists who are more invested in their own independent growth than the concerns that are perpetually tied to any prescriptive ideology. This has no doubt raised their autonomy, and to such a degree that the emphasis on the work's critical reception has become preferable to the past dispute over whether "ceramic" is a legitimate medium. And while most of Leuthold's contemporaries are focused on their own contributions to the canon of Western art history, his work seems to extrapolate and spin off from the Far East, with its philosophical attributes that least stress the notion of assertive individualism. At the same time, his work has to be seen as a personal negotiation rather than a literal or even ironic appropriation, which often is considered the norm by today's popular consensus. Not to mention the tension it would create if one were to place Leuthold's work in the context of cultural production and the whole global economy of art, which has elevated the democratic values of late capitalism while marginalizing most of the indigenous cultures, whose lineages benefit from an unbroken continuity of tradition. And yet, multiculturalism has opened up possibilities for artists from non-European cultures to focus on the resources that derive from their own cultural heritages.

By the beginning of the twentieth century in the West, the attempt to actualize hermetic and alchemical vehicles as means of cultural transformation had already been established, after emerging from nineteenth century occultism and Theosophy generated by Rudolf Steiner, Gurdjieff, Fulcanelli, Jung, and the Eranos Gnostics like Corbin, Scholem, and Eliade. John Perreault, in an insightful essay, suggested that Leuthold's discovery of the writings of the Christian mystic and theologian Jacob Boehme was revelatory to his own sensitive nature.[1] He wrote that, similar to Boehme's various mystical experiences throughout his youth—which culminated one day in 1600 when he was able to conceive his vision of the spiritual structure of the world through the exquisite beauty of a beam of sunlight reflected in a pewter dish—Leuthold has created an equivalent of intricately carved sculptures that at once evokes an intrinsic relationship between forms that embrace the ephemeral lightness among objects in nature and the absolute attention to details, through which he constructs the entire composition. One can also recall the Austrian physicist and philosopher Ernst Mach's recognition of sensation as a legible type of phenomenalism. As he wrote in his youth, "The superfluity of the role played by the 'thing-in-itself' abruptly dawned upon me. On a bright summer day in the open air, the world with my ego suddenly appeared to me as one coherent mass of sensations, only more strongly coherent in the ego."

Similarly, Robert Fludd's macrocosm-microcosm analogy, a theory in which all occurrences in the microcosm (man) are influenced by the macrocosm (the heavens), applied to his discussion on the circulation of the blood—the heart is the sun and the blood is like the circulating planets. Whatever were the means of creating a new culture of Hermeticism in opposition to Cartesianism that evolved Newtonian and Darwinian sciences, which led to the rise of industrialism, there have been those few who refuse to be part of the mechanistic dualism or rationalism. This of course leads to other references that bare similar synthesis of men and nature, at least in the Western hermetic and alchemical tradition, as I have mentioned, which is that of the Eastern evocation that seems clear in the installation *Field*, made while Leuthold was in residence at Fuping, China, in 2007: Two horses, standing on a relatively low pedestal, bracket a symmetrical arrangement of three small symbolic abstract forms of Buddhist temples, with one row of three circular bundles of ropes carefully laid at the head of nearly thirty large white wheels placed in succession right behind them, concluding in a group of at least fifty smaller cones of a variety of colors. *Field* thereby suggests a chariot formation, inspired by the burial sites in Xi'an (the ancient capital of China, 221 B.C. to A.D. 907) of Shaanxi province, that were discovered in 1974, which include chariots, wheels, vessels, horses, soldiers, and many other objects. In keeping up with the old techniques of tri-color lead glazes, usually pigmented with copper for green, cobalt for blue, and manganese for dark violet, with the addition of a brighter blue and a rich iron honey glaze, Leuthold also adapts the regal and ceremonial procession that rekindles the monumental scale of the Xi'an sites, while at the same time recontextualizing his assertion in contemporary art history.

Leuthold's circular form of the landmark wheels, similarly, represents an ongoing repertoire of renewable, self-generating sets of imagery that rely on the simultaneity of things in flux and things centered. Again, apart from making direct reference to the Neolithic *bi* discs that were placed in tombs along with other objects that the tomb's inhabitants wished to bring with them into the afterlife, they also allude to the mandala—a universal symbol of sacred geometry that appears in its multitude of variations, from Islamic art, in the knot works of the ancient Celts, in the sand paintings of the Tibetan and Navajo (Diné) cultures, to the sacred art of Christian mystics—where the center and circumference are in complete harmony. While the latter is a form without beginning or end suggesting wholeness, completeness, and the cyclical nature of life, the former equivocally typifies endless potential and movement outward of the one toward the many, the heart of all life force, and so on. The occasional holes in the middle are the open spaces for the descended soul to travel through from earth to heaven.

Leuthold's mandala-like constructions also suggest another reference: that of Bruce Conner's exploitation of afterimages, particularly in his dense interweaving of black and white contemporaneous drawings, which began with *Kenwood Avenue*, then continued right onto his legendary *Mandala* series of the mid 1960s. They are generally composed of several concentric circles that form a central mandala, which result in a stunning optical fibrillation that, on the one hand, resembles a cell seen under a microscope. On the other hand, the tension that accelerates between the dense black inked lines and the exposed whiteness of the paper is a form of controlled randomization, which in turn exudes an intense spatial disorientation that evolves ever so slowly to our visual reception. But for Conner, the whole concern of his *Mandala* drawings has always coincided with his manipulation of the contrast between black and white that causes a sense of perpetual flux known as "persistence of vision"—a phenomenon of the eye by which an afterimage is thought to persist for approximately one twenty-fifth of a second on the retina, a time usually associated with filmic sequences. Thus, its alchemy is one that resembles an altered state of awareness.

Conversely, in Leuthold's construction of his own mandala, the generating light from the center to the outer edges is more akin to organic structure that occurs in nature. Moreover, quite opposite to Conner's more fractured and dispersed imagery, Leuthold's spatial sensibility is fairly consistent and fluid, despite the swirling lines that constitute a great sense of movement, almost like a vortex where the speed and rate of rotation are more pronounced at the center and decrease progressively toward the edges. Still, each line gets thicker and further apart from one another as it reveals its sensuous folds. There is a hypnotic sense of calmness in each of Leuthold's wheels, partly because of the way in which the artist's sense of touch is barely dictated by gravity or the pressure of hands, and partly because he allows his personal sense of form and irregularity to be analogous to natural forms or living organisms that are preconditioned to response stimuli, reproduction, growth and development, and maintenance of homoeostasis as a stable whole. This is the reason why the wheels, discs, and hemispheres are, in essence, generative to the cones, stacks, dyads, and receptors.

Site-specifically created, and installed for the first time on the occasion of his first retrospective of fifteen years of work, Leuthold's *Offering* is the artist's largest-scaled installation to date. It reveals his ability to bring a wide range of invented forms into one cohesive display that applies to various functions. From utilizing different treatments of fairly unconventional pedestals with those that either hang off the ceiling, suspended in mid-air like a constellation, or rest carefully on thin metal rods, to mixing a variety of heights and spacing of the pedestals on the floor and walls for his selections of *Lines* works and *Receptors*, the exhibit is uniformly cohesive and stimulating. On one level, by reducing the physical nature of conventional pedestals, Leuthold has gained a greater freedom in the placement of the works as a group, insofar as the manipulation of intervals is conducive to the addition and subtraction that is required in adapting to different given spaces. On another level, these variable formal choices create opportunities to facilitate necessary and visceral structures that are commendable to the artist's vision.

By rising above the floor surface in their long, cylindrical stalks with different heights, the two cone installations appear like lotus flowers with many personifications of Zephyr, blowing west wind to the invisible Venus, who, born in the sea foam, is wafted on a scallop shell to her sacred island Cyprus, where the nymph Pomona, descended from the ancient goddess of fruit trees, runs to meet her with a brocade mantle. *Offering* evokes both a sense of serenity, which is that of Leuthold's long interest in Eastern philosophy, and the lyrical power of Greek mythology. (Both refer to the genesis of Theosophy.) What it proposes is the synthesis that infuses creative power and purity amid adverse surroundings with the Neoplatonic belief in the soul as ascendable toward a union with god through contemplation of beauty. Coincidently, both aspects share the similar reminder of the miracle of beauty (love) and light (life), which in an emotional context, could be useful to both a spiritual and practical understanding of Tao (the world and our place in it), as well as a Platonic and Hermetic unification.

Right at the center of the gallery, above the floor surface, is the constellation of a multitude of bent, irregular wheels, composed as one symmetrical unit in contrast to the two asymmetrical cone structures on either side below. Here the interplay of the formal symmetry of the ecclesial and the pairing of the asymmetry of typography is, in fact, in succinct equilibrium. Not only do they correspond to one another on a perfect pitch of arrangement, resulting from Leuthold's invented supports, they also are susceptible to movement, and intended to exude a sense of generous space and atmosphere, for which lightness is perpetually negotiating with density. Nowhere do we see a forced hierarchy upon the way in which Leuthold conceives his work, nor do we detect any form of discrimination within the installation as a whole. Not that surprisingly, the past thirty years of works that is built on a desire for universal embrace of all things equal, a balance of men and nature, is evident throughout the exhibition. This is a political act of "non-violent" philosophy, which couldn't be more timely applied, as reiterated with the inclusion of Coretta Scott King's text, an excerpt from her *My Life with Martin Luther King, Jr.* In essence, reality and healing along with transformation and creation lie in the in-between, which Leuthold suggests we all must maintain.

-Phong Bui

1. John Perreault, "The Center Holds," in *Marc Leuthold: The Center Holds* (Westerfield, OH: The American Ceramic Society, 2003), 10-13.

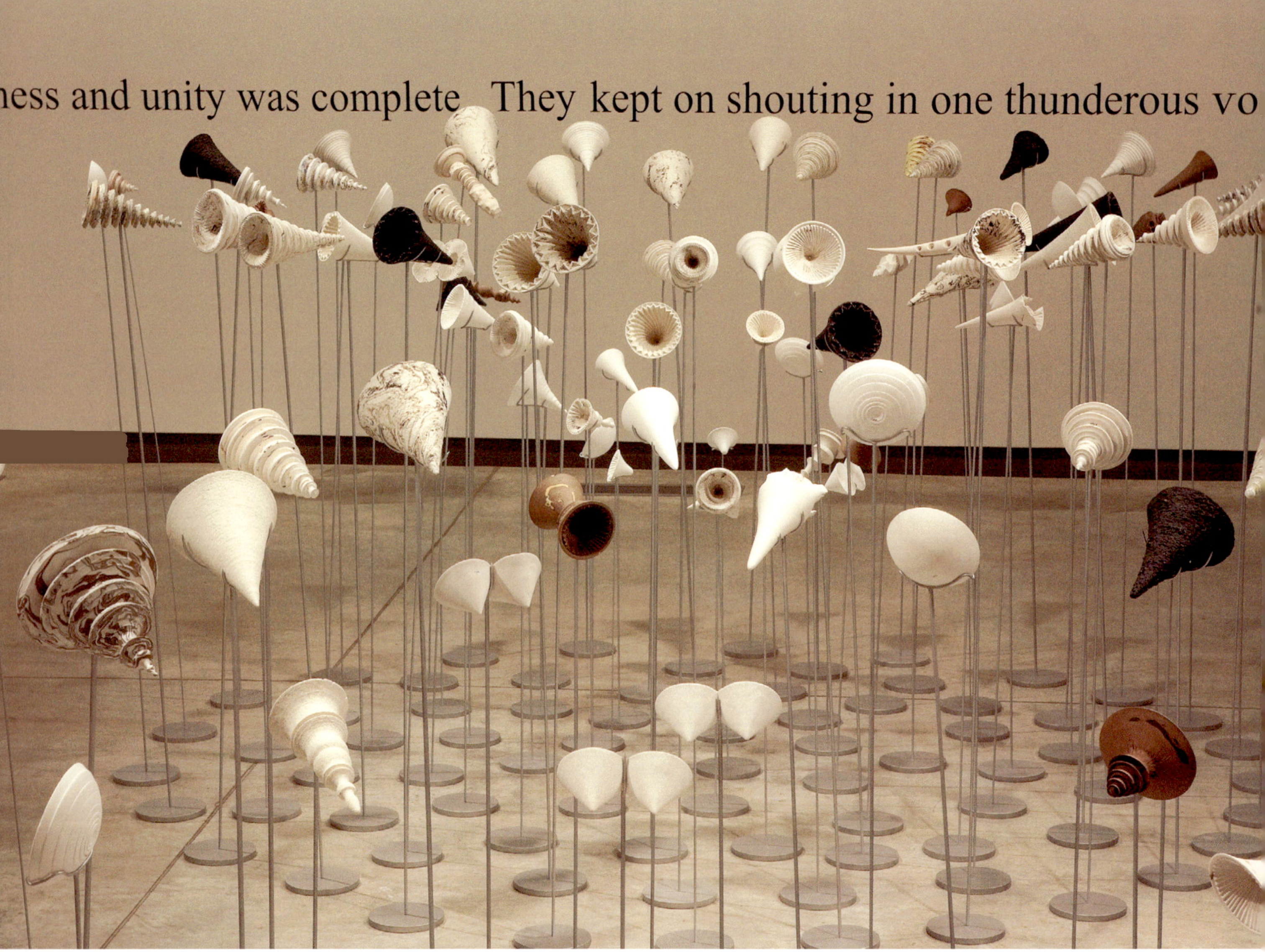

Installation view of *Offering,* Daum Museum of Contemporary Art, February 2010.

Offering: Marc Leuthold

Walking into Marc Leuthold's exhibition, *Offering*, at the Daum Museum of Contemporary Art in Sedalia, Missouri, US, one is confronted by an enormous, light-filled gallery, its white walls bisected by a line of evocative text quoting Coretta Scott King's description of the impact one of Martin Luther King's speeches had on his audience. It reads:

> I have a dream that my four little children one day will live in a nation where they will not be judged by the color of their skin, but by the content of their character.... This will be the day when all of God's children will be able to sing with new meaning. When we allow freedom to ring from every town and every hamlet from every state and every city, we will be able to speed up that day when all of God's children, black men and white men, Jews and Gentiles, Protestants and Catholics, will be able to join hands and sing in the words of the old Negro spiritual, 'Free at last! Free at last! Great God A-mighty, we are free at last!' As Martin ended, there was an awed silence that is the greatest tribute an orator can be paid. And then a tremendous crash of sound as two hundred and fifty thousand people shouted in ecstatic accord with his words. The feeling that they had of oneness and unity was complete. They kept on shouting in one thunderous voice, and for that brief moment the Kingdom of God seemed to have come on earth.[1]

This quotation, which is a visual component of the exhibition, is reflected upon in Leuthold's artist's statement. In it, he poses the following questions: "Do even good leaders become part of a dark system that has gradually weakened our country? What can we do to help ourselves? When does it become our duty to take back our government?" His stunning *Offering* is an attempt to "call attention to these questions."

The beauty of the quotation's content is augmented by the fact that the text is stark black against sterile, white walls. In this context, the ordinariness of the colors black and white becomes a metaphor for race, societal dissonance and the urgent hope for harmony that serves as a literal and conceptual frame around the installation.

At the front of the gallery, displayed on polished grey concrete floors that stretch like an ocean of integration between the black of the text and the white of the walls, are two groupings of ceramic shapes. Their forms evoke the loudspeakers of the civil rights movement, or ancient horns used to call martial warnings, funnels, cones, shells or animal's protective tusks. They rest on delicate, linear metal stands that range in height from twenty-four inches to fifty inches. Made from many different kinds of clay, the coloration of the forms moves subtly from grays, to ochre, to blacks, to browns, suggesting all the ranges of pigmentation of human skin.

The artist was inspired to make these forms by an incident that took place during the Nara Period in Japan during the eighth century. Leuthold writes, "(I)n A.D. 764, as an act of atonement, Empress Shotoku commissioned one million wooden, conically shaped pagoda forms, each containing a scroll of Buddhist scripture called the *Daranikyo sutra* (*Dharani*)…It was believed that this gesture would help a worried people get through bad times."

Leuthold's cones are presented tilting slightly upward as if looking heavenward. Each is subtly different from the next and yet in aggregate they make, "a diverse group, a population." The simplicity of their forms belies the manifold metaphors that they evoke. A cone resembles a horn, an instrument historically used to call for help. The archangel Gabriel blows his horn on Judgment Day to herald the beginning of change. The Jews sound the traditional shofar, or ram's horn, on high holy days to announce the start of a period of sacredness and purity. Both interpretations are relevant to the exhibition because the grouping of cones has a distinct figurative poetry suggestive of a grouping of souls, waiting together to be called to the better days described so eloquently in the quotation by Martin Luther King Jr. But the forms of these cones are open and non-literal, thus allowing viewers to dream other meanings into them. When seen as shells, their meaning changes because shells are homes, shields used to protect against the vicissitudes of the ocean's currents. And like shell-dwellers, each human needs a place to be safe from the cultural currents that buffet us. When viewed as funnels the meaning again opens and shifts to express the fact that each person experiences a surfeit of occurrences in a lifetime, which must be taken in slowly, organized and distilled, drop by drop, into the unique narrative that defines who we believe ourselves to be. The forms Leuthold has created also bring to mind the loudspeaker, an image both malevolent (when associated with police brutality and oppression) and courageous (when connected to demonstrators for civil rights).

The fact that there are two groupings of these beautiful, small sculptures augments the theme of binary that infuses the exhibition. Each evocation that the sculptures conjure contains an opposition: the horn calls for positive change and punitive judgment, the shell protects against vulnerability but shields against experience, the funnel organizes but stems the flow, the loudspeaker calls to action but also threatens and cajoles. Just as the text on the wall becomes a visual duality, describing a call for oneness, so also is there hope, and its opposite, within the complex simplicity of these clay shapes.

The surfaces on these clay sculptures are varied. Some are utterly smooth, while others are carved by hand into spiral-like tusks. In many cultures, the spiral connotes the endless repetition of societal error. In Leuthold's sure hands, the carving is both earthy embellishment and calligraphic cipher. Some of the forms' interiors have subtle, delicate colors such as purples, blues and yellows, body colors blooming with bruising and mortality. Some look blackened and burned. Some are broken or mangled. They range in scale from about three inches to twenty-four inches and sway lightly on their delicate stands. Each "character" is unique, handmade without a template and yet as a mass they are integrated. In short, these are ceramic portraits of souls, or voices, visual representations of human complexity, subtlety, beauty and originality. They become representative

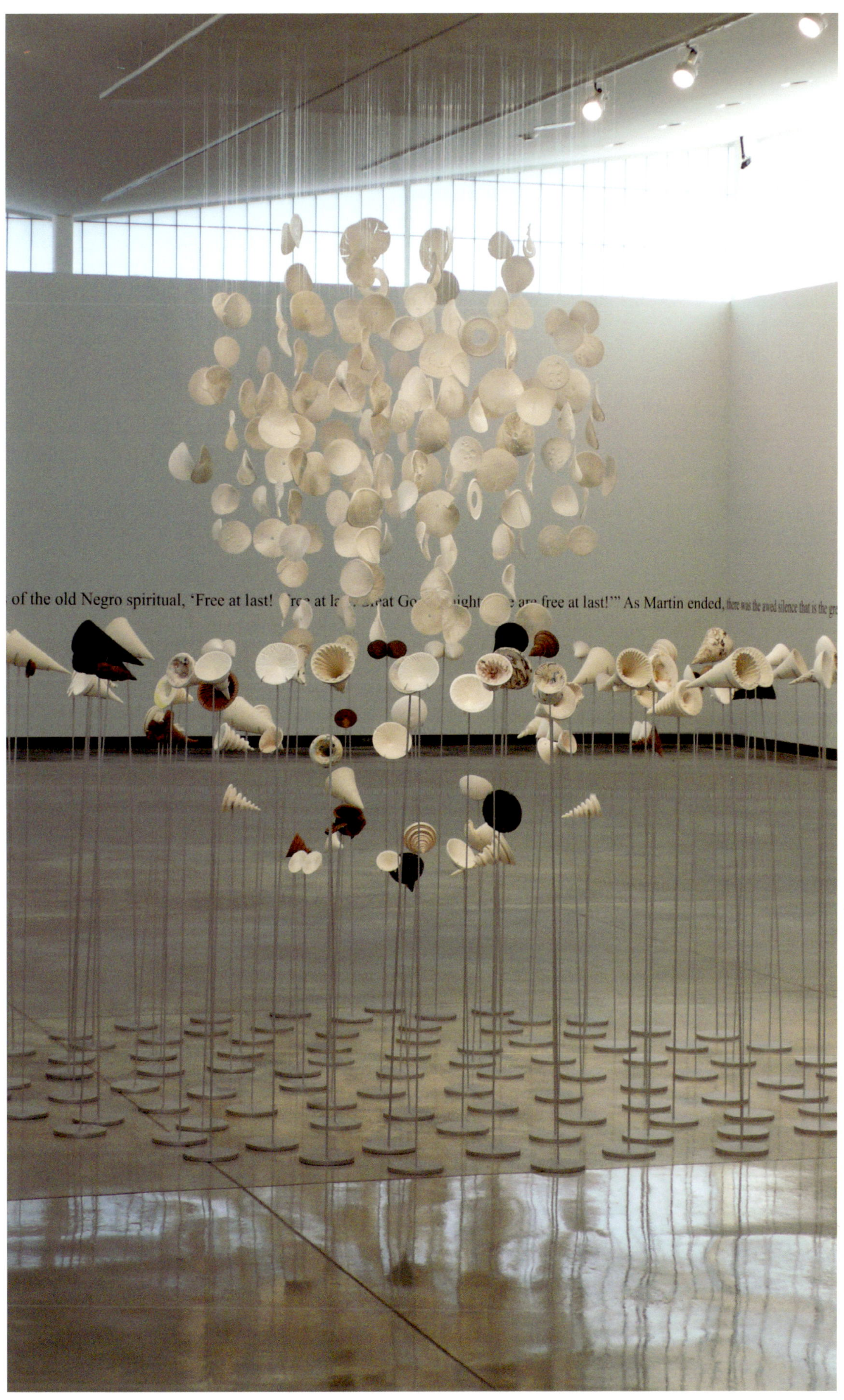
of the old Negro spiritual, 'Free at last!
free at last!'" As Martin ended, there was the awed silence that is the

Installation view of *Offering* (detail), at
Daum Museum of Contemporary Art, February 2010.

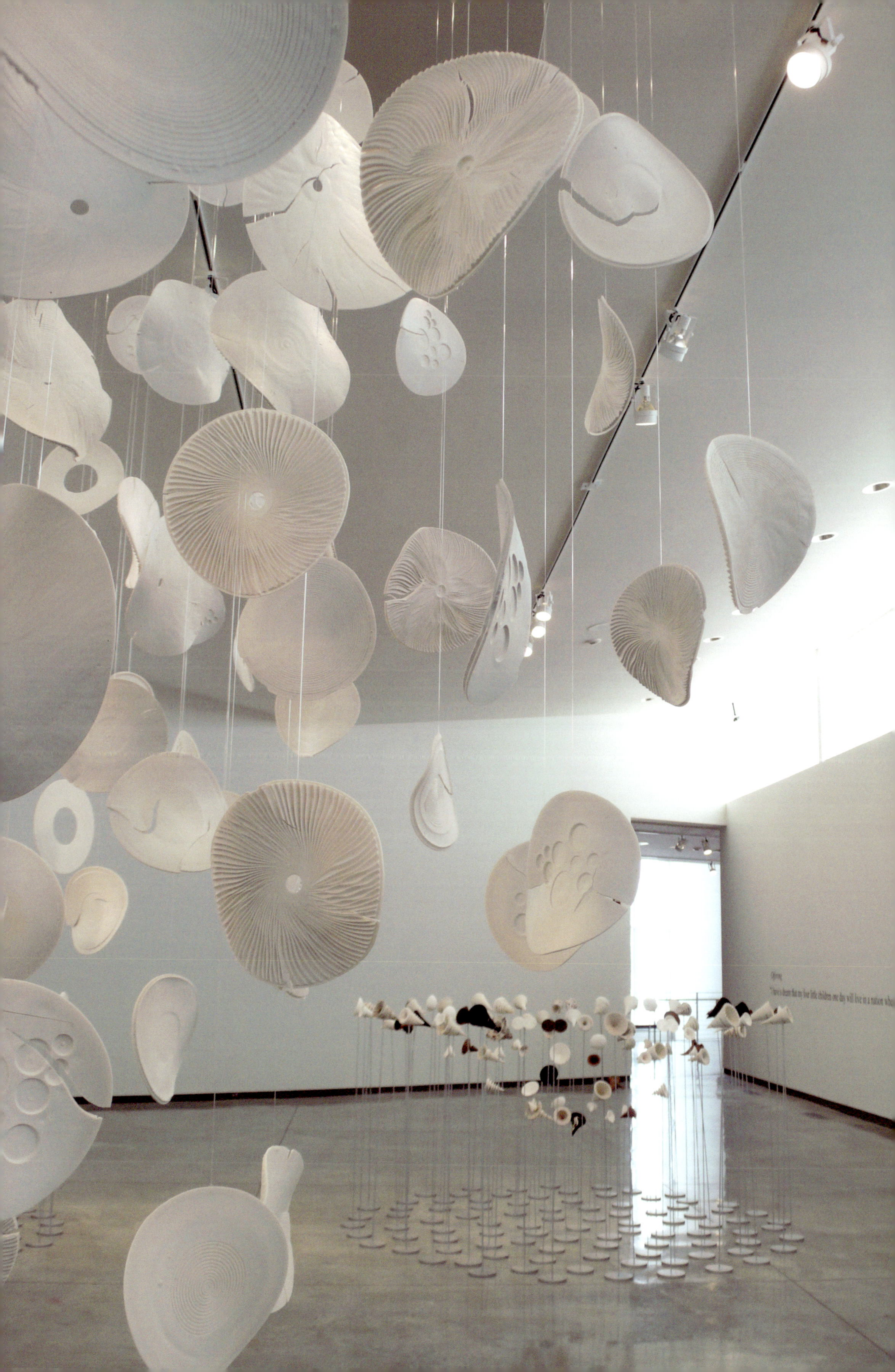

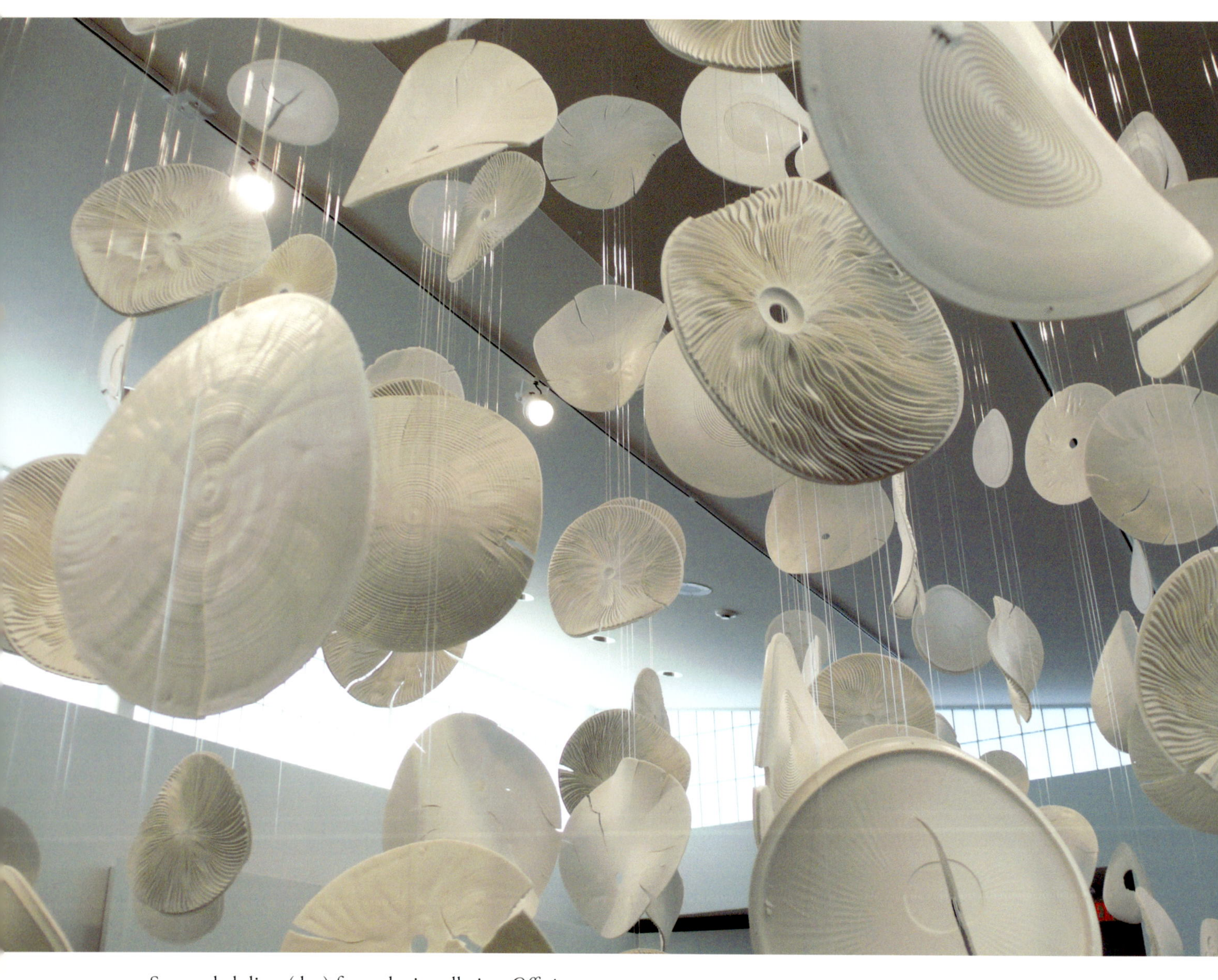

Suspended discs (day) from the installation *Offering*, at Daum Museum of Contemporary Art, February 2010.

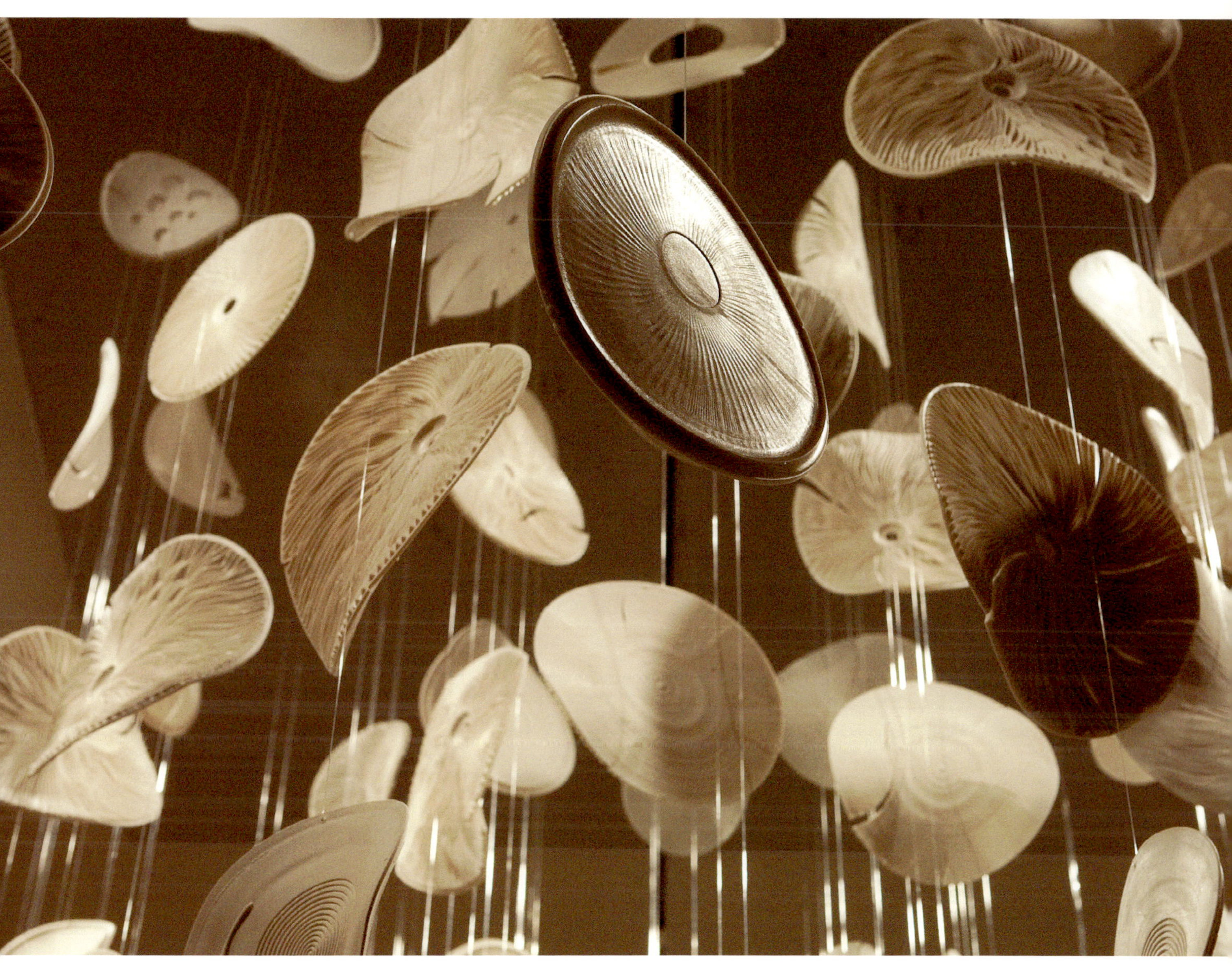

Suspended discs (night) from the installation *Offering*, at Daum Museum of Contemporary Art, February 2010.

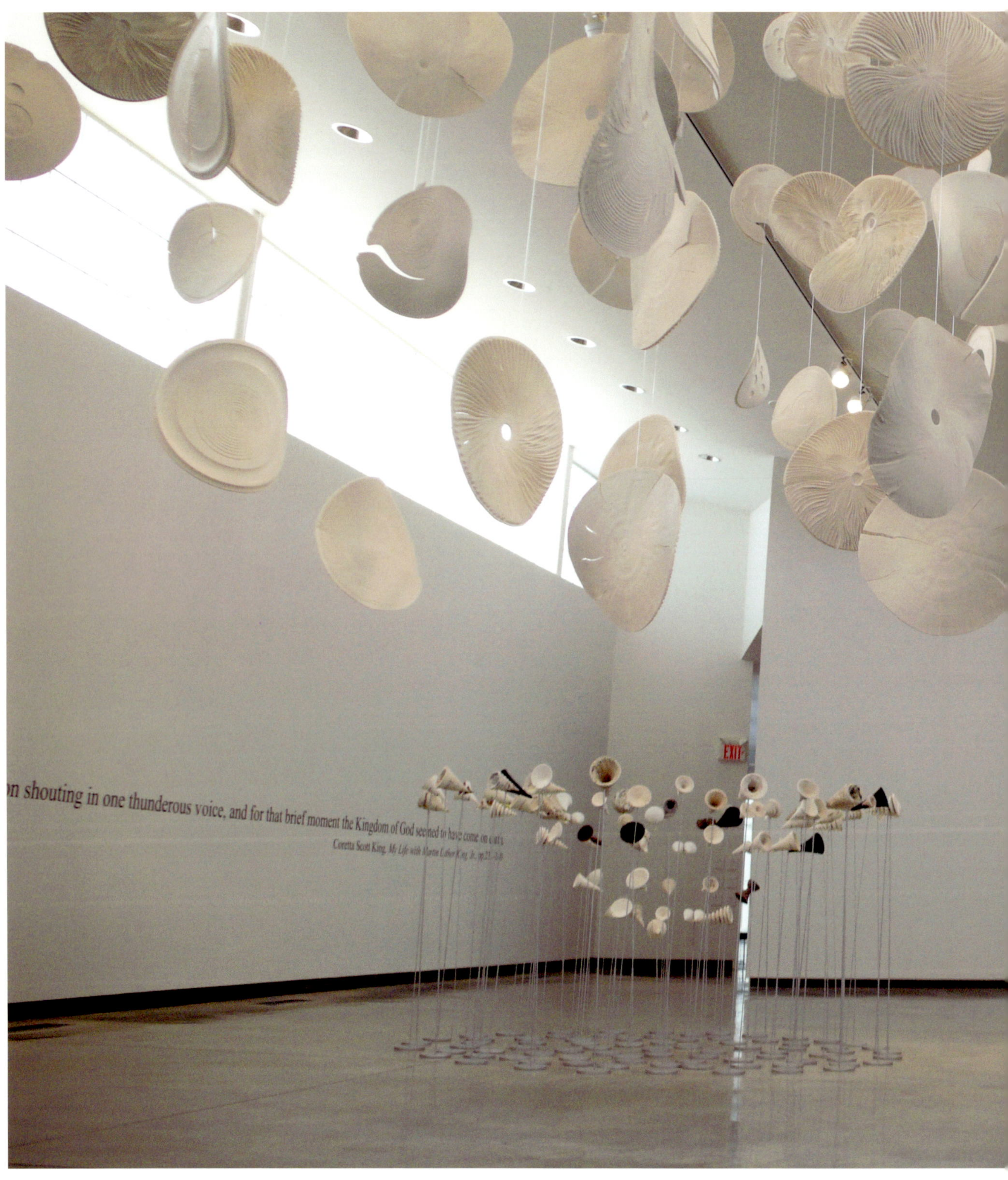
shouting in one thunderous voice, and for that brief moment the Kingdom of God seemed to have come on
Coretta Scott King, *My Life with Martin Luther King, Jr.*
EXIT

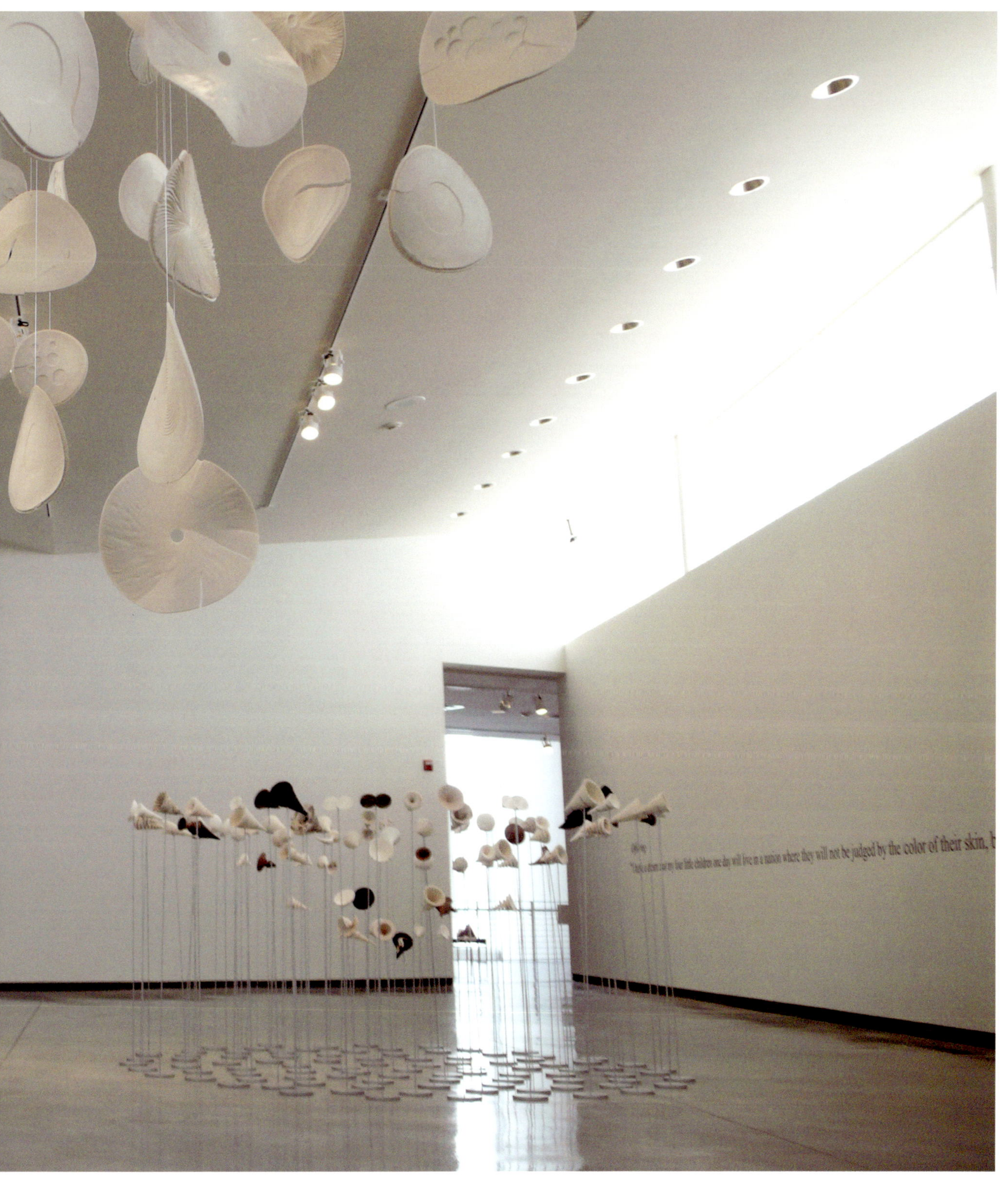
a nation where they will not be judged by the color of their skin,

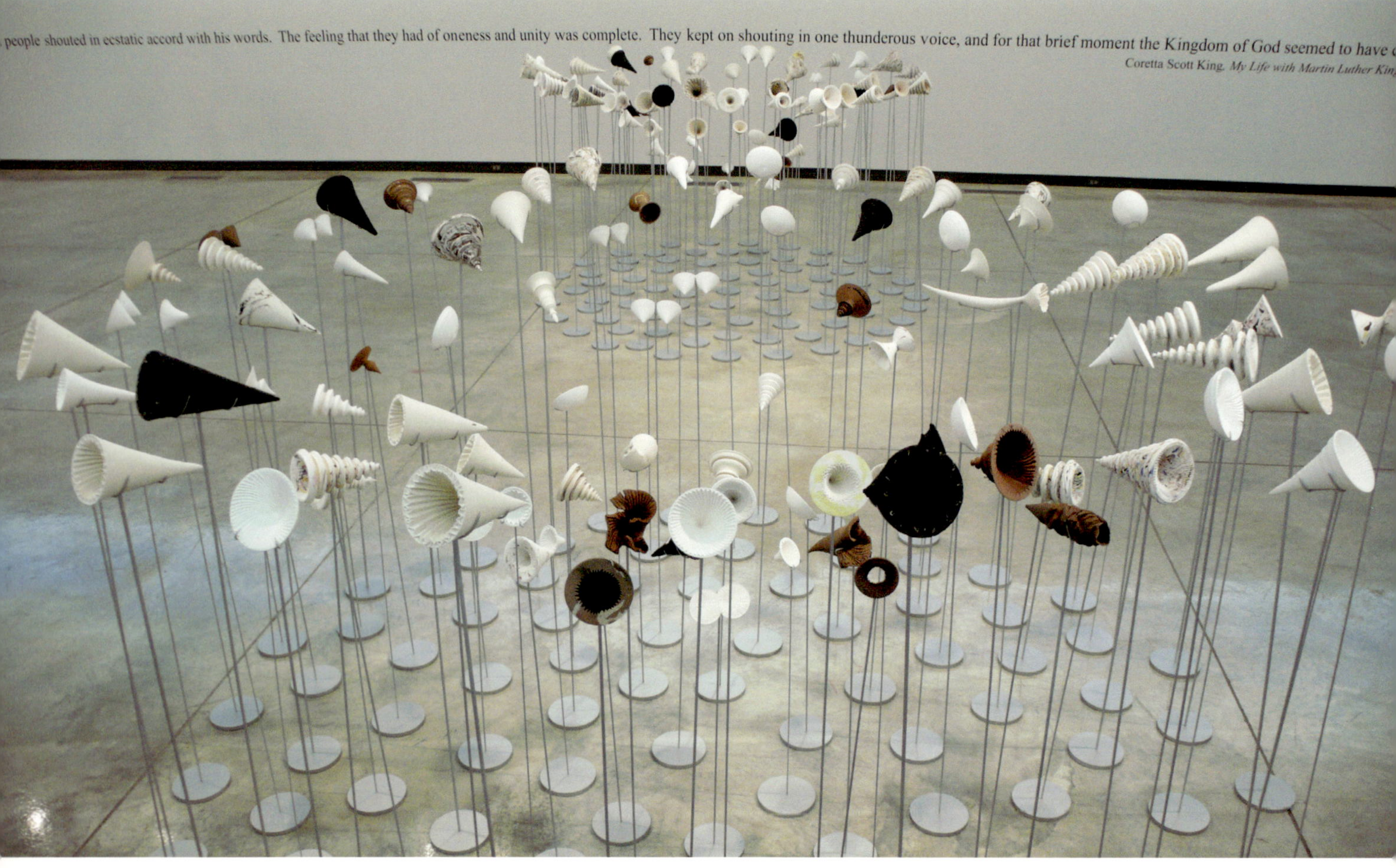

Detail of the installation *Offering*, on view at Daum Museum of Contemporary Art, February 2010.

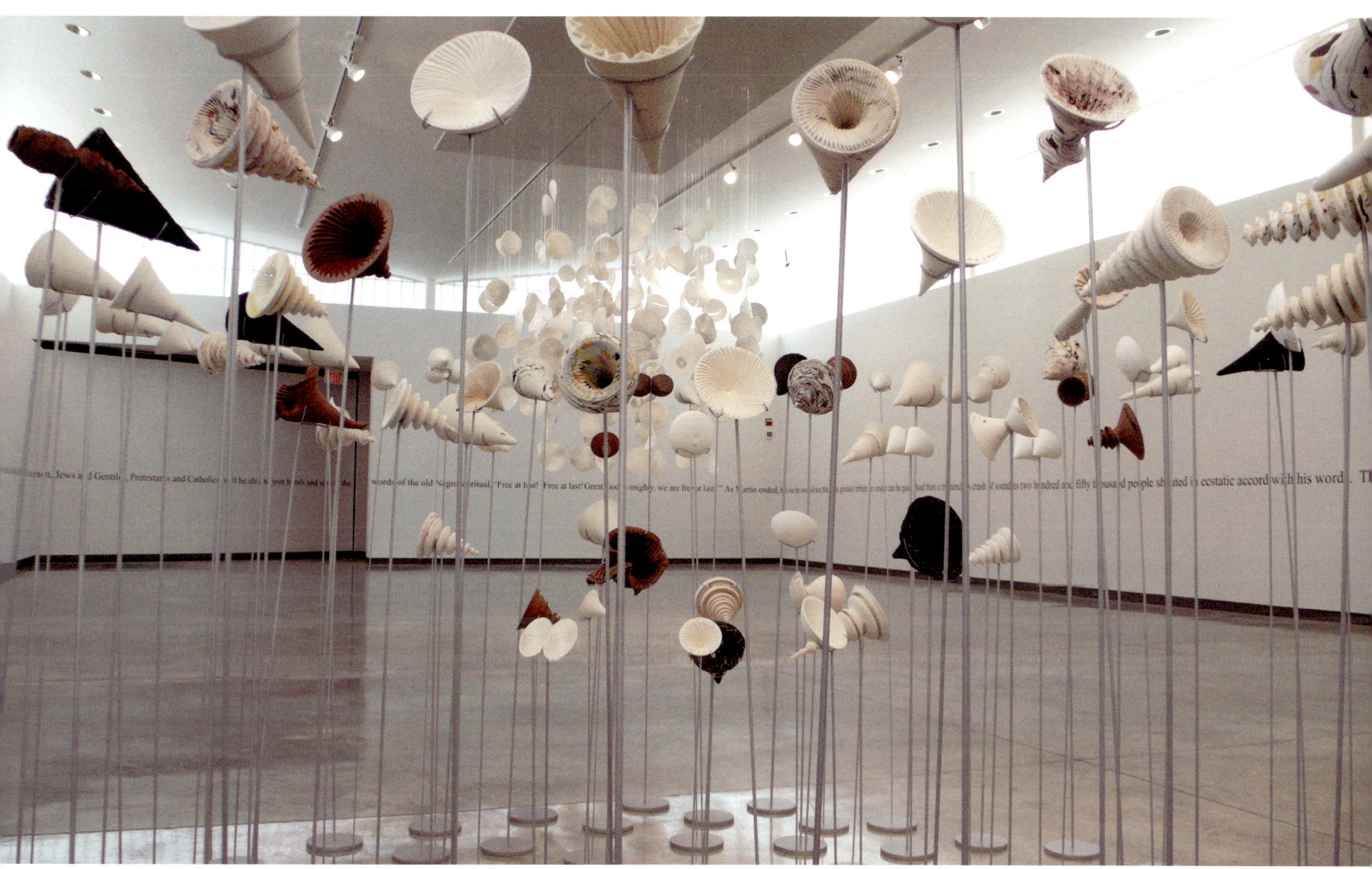

Detail of the installation *Offering*,
on view at Daum Museum of Contemporary Art, 2010.

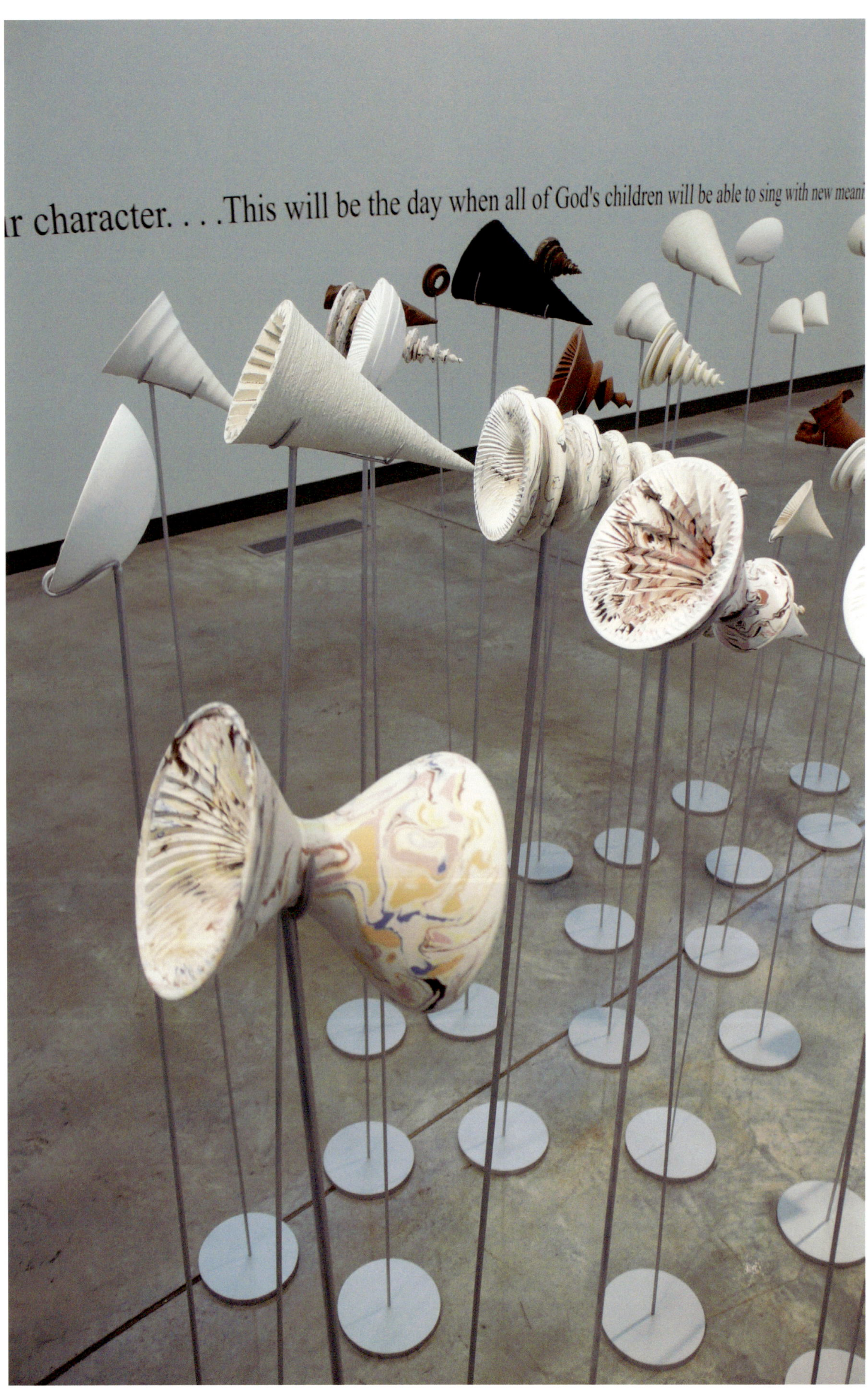
r character. . . .This will be the day when all of God's children will be able to sing with new meani

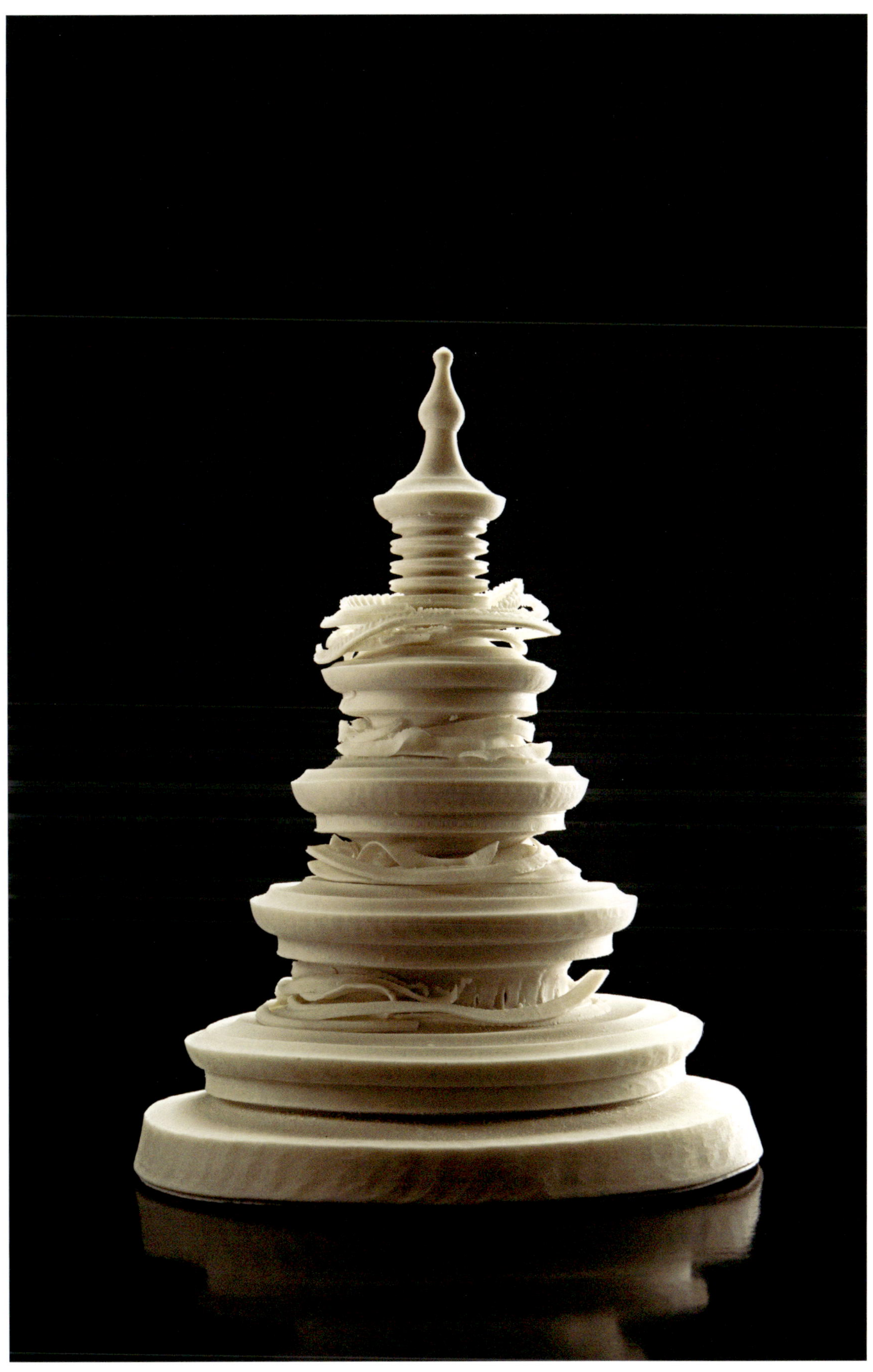

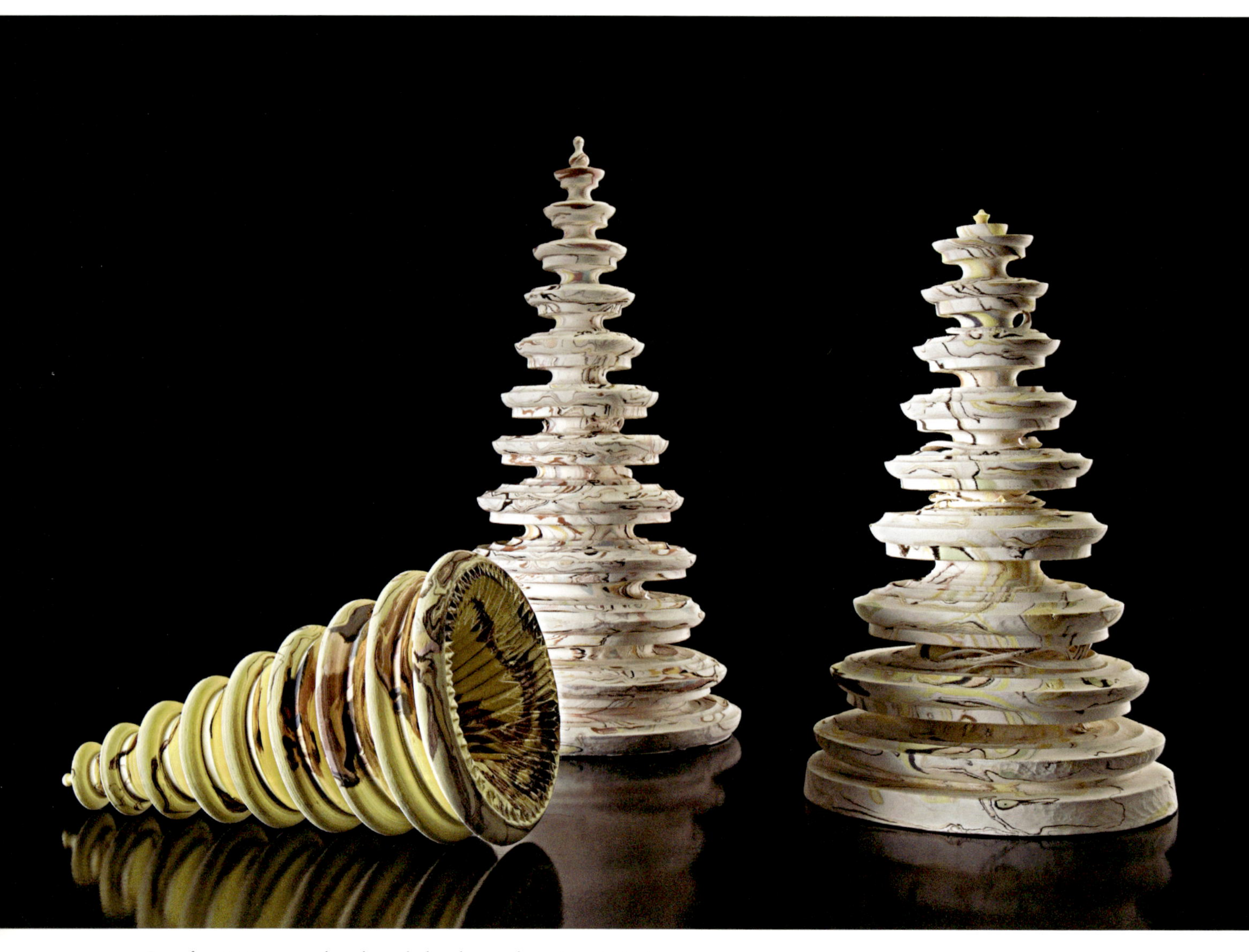

Pagodas, 2009, carved and marbelized porcelain, 10 x 17 x 9 in.

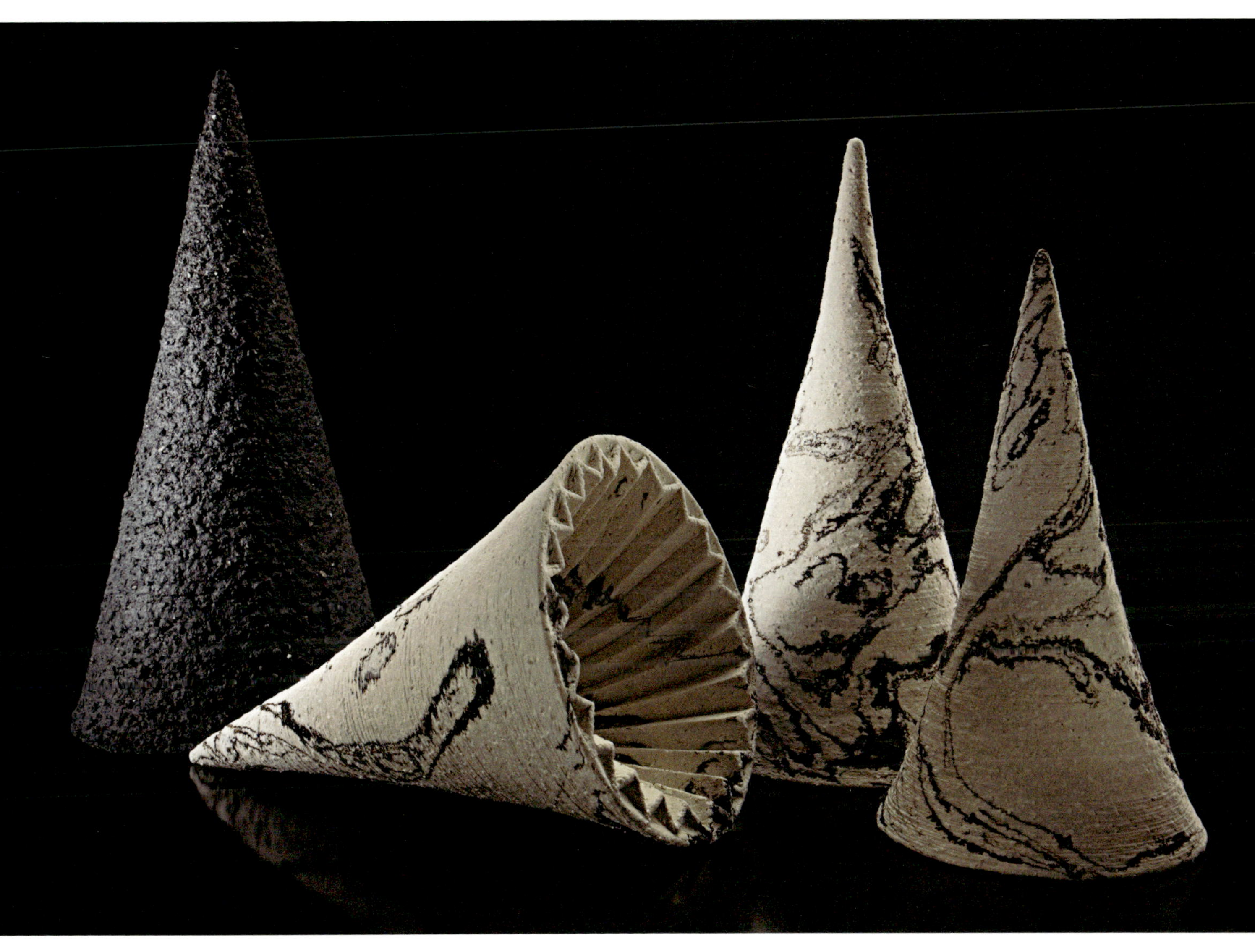

Cones, 2009, marbelized stoneware, 9 1/2 x 16 x 8 in.

Cones (Hades), 2009, unglazed stoneware, 9 x 4 x 4 in.

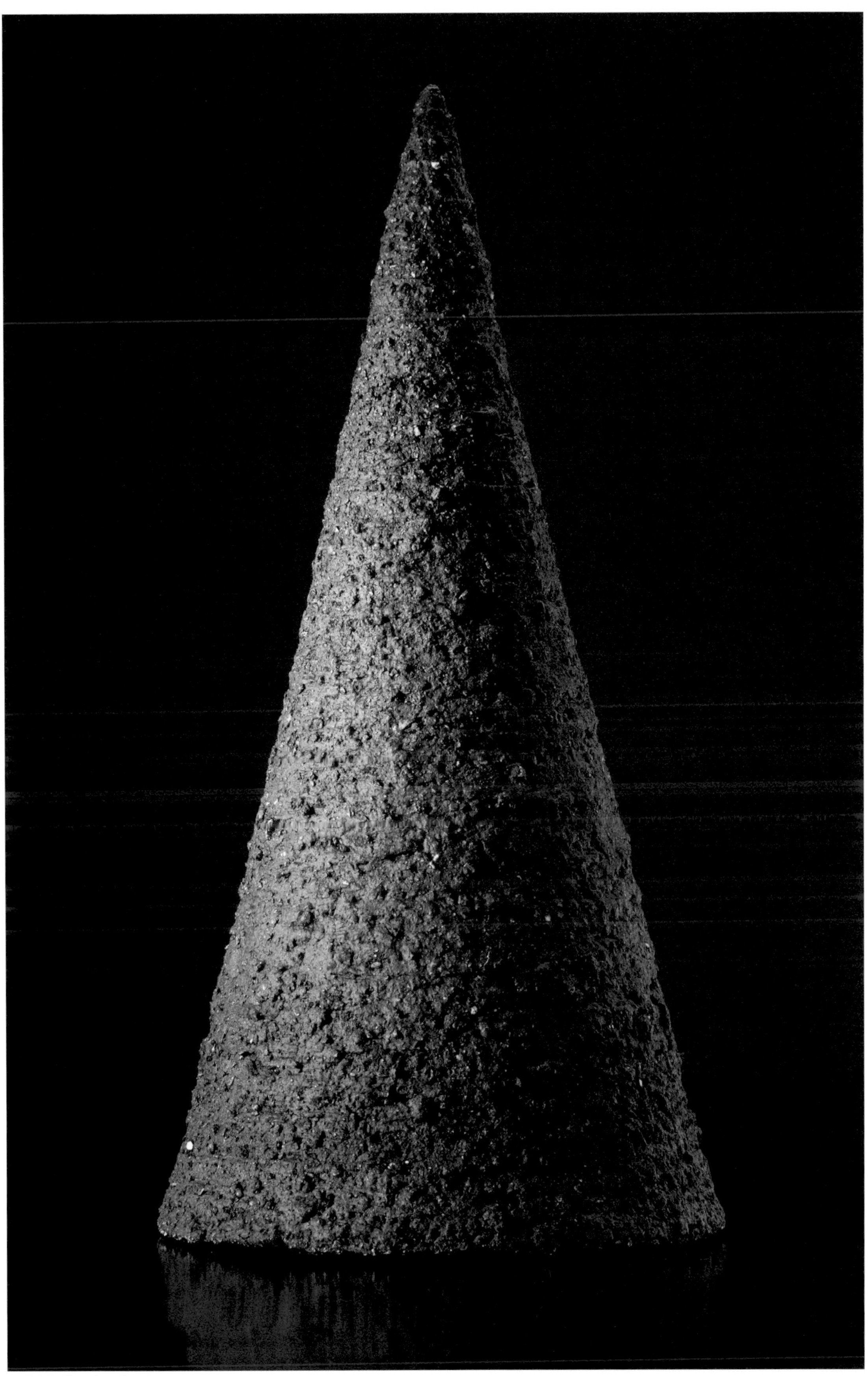

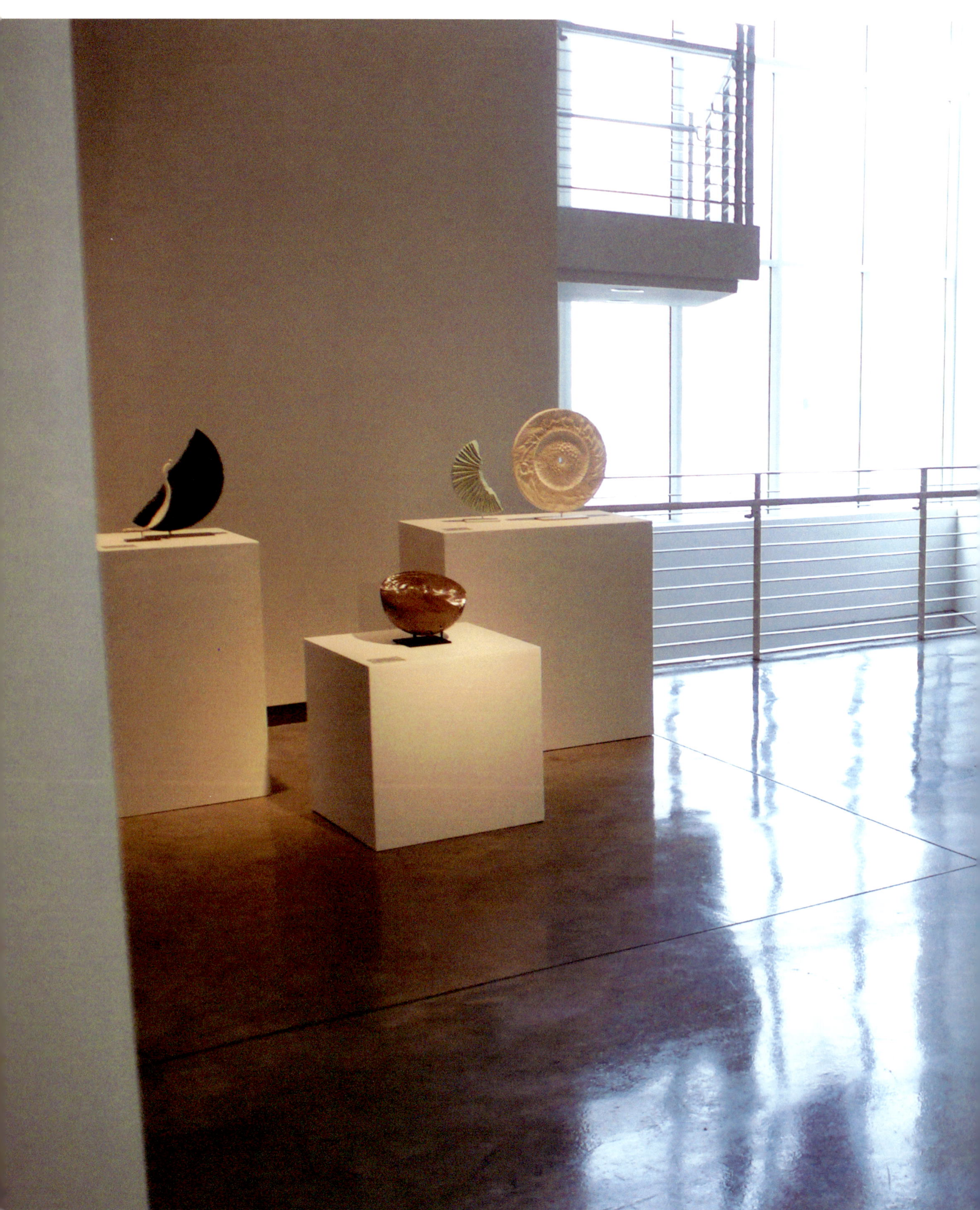

Installation view of the exhibition *Marc Leuthold, Sculpture, 1995-2010*

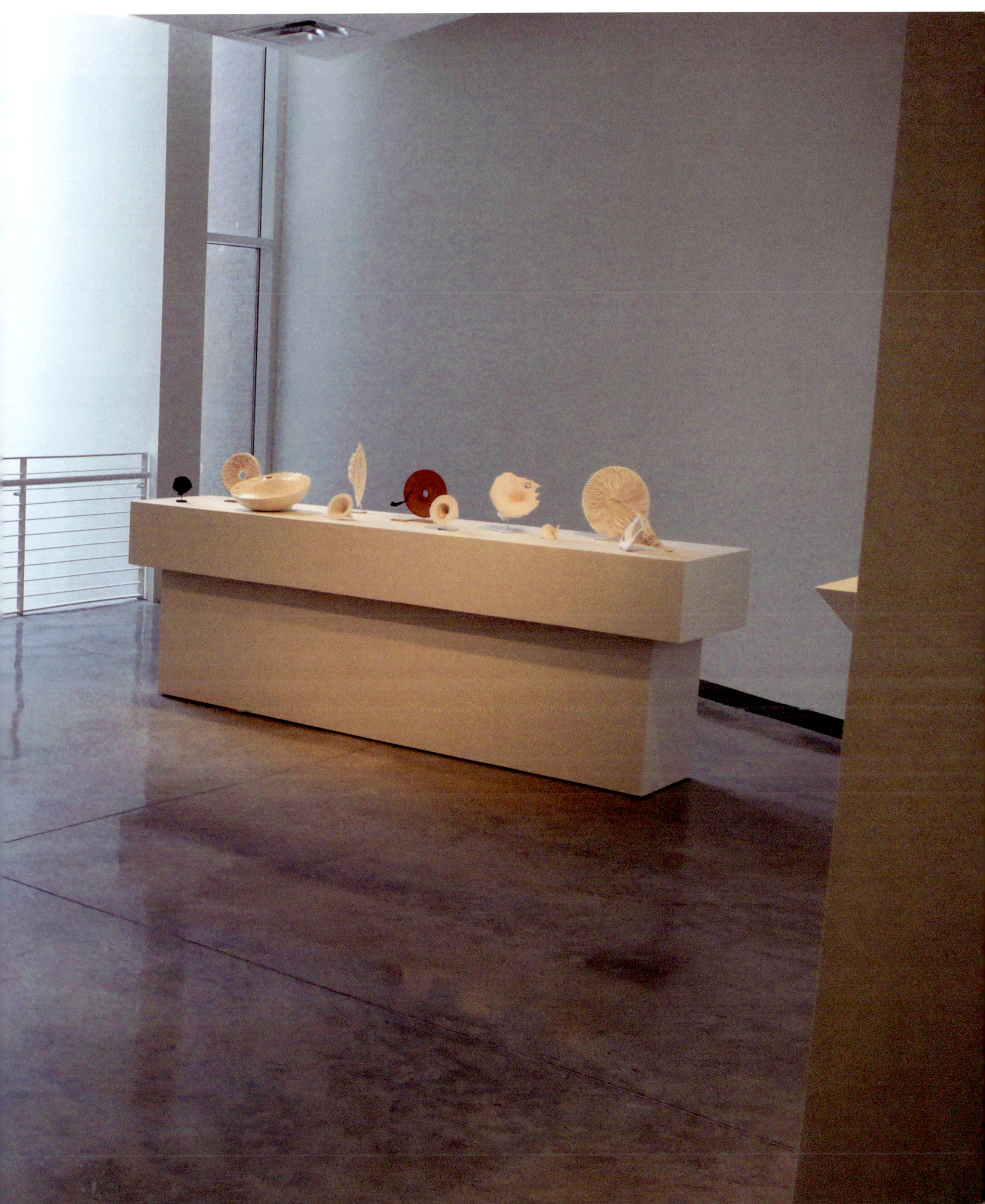

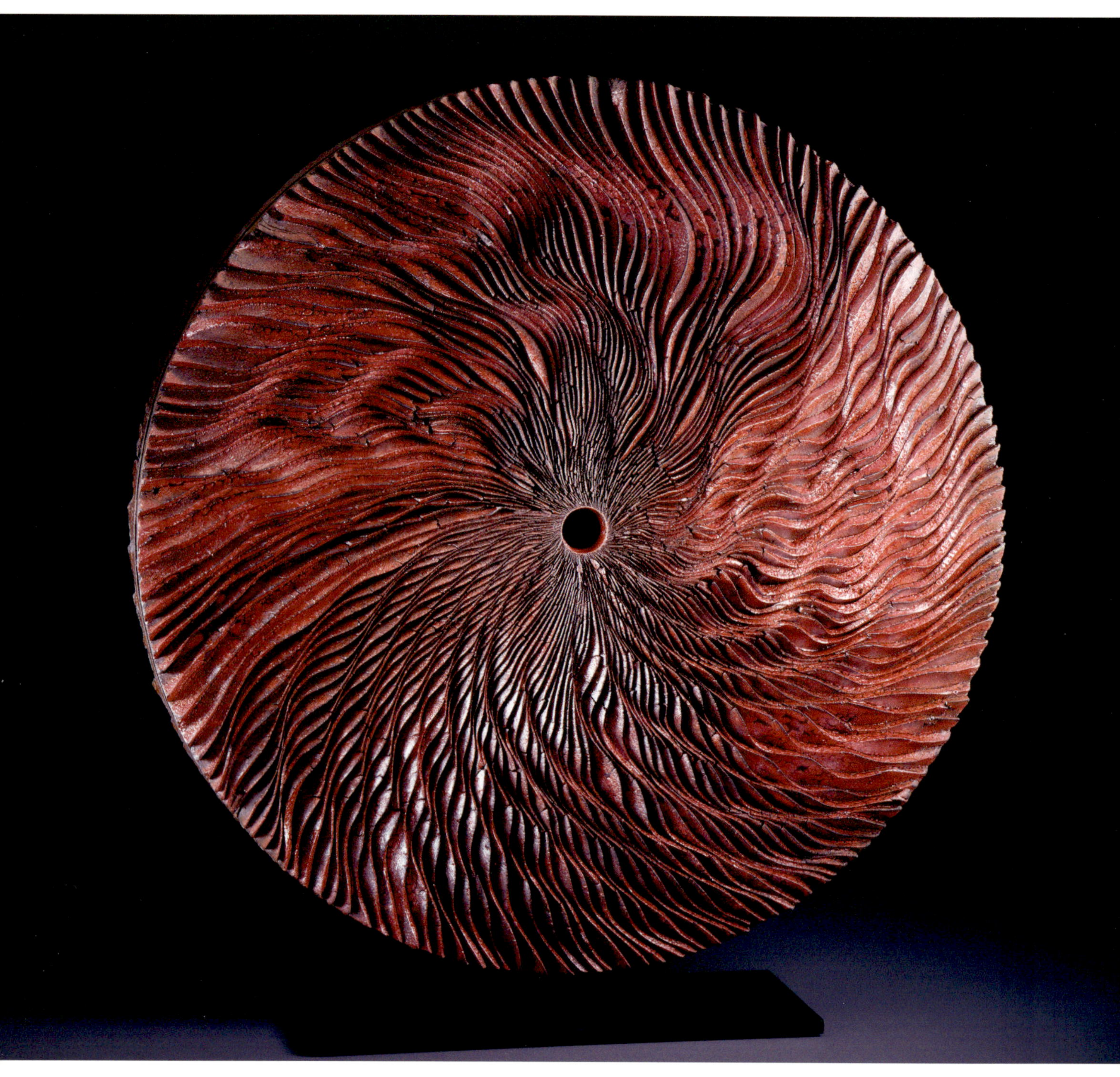

Boehme (Red), side B, 1998-99, glazed earthenware, 17 in. diam. x 2 in.

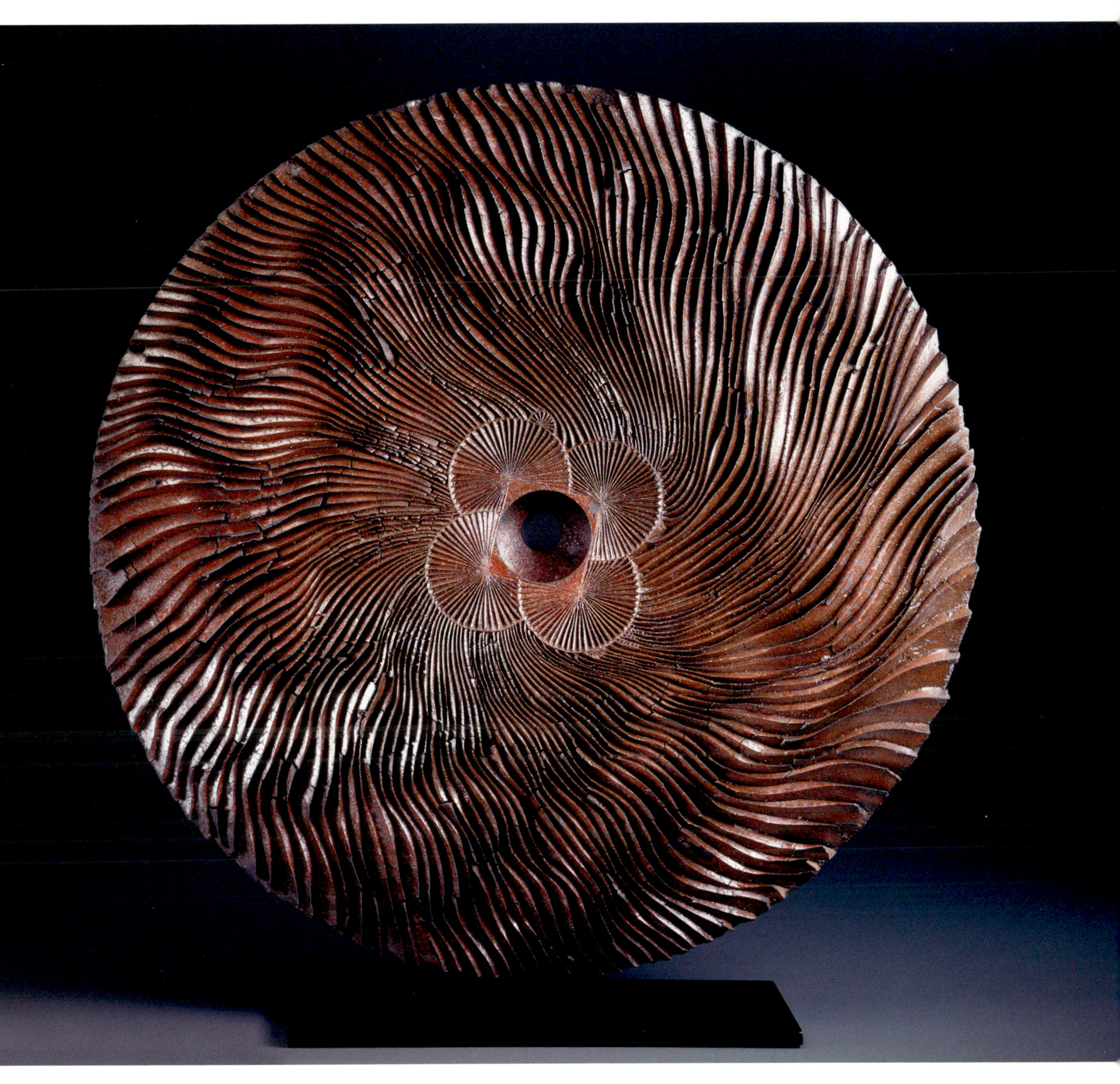

Boehme (Red), side A, 1998-99, glazed earthenware, 17 in. diam. x 2 in.

Demi, 2001-04, glazed and unglazed stoneware, 15 x 9 x 2 in.; 9 x 7 x 1/2 in.

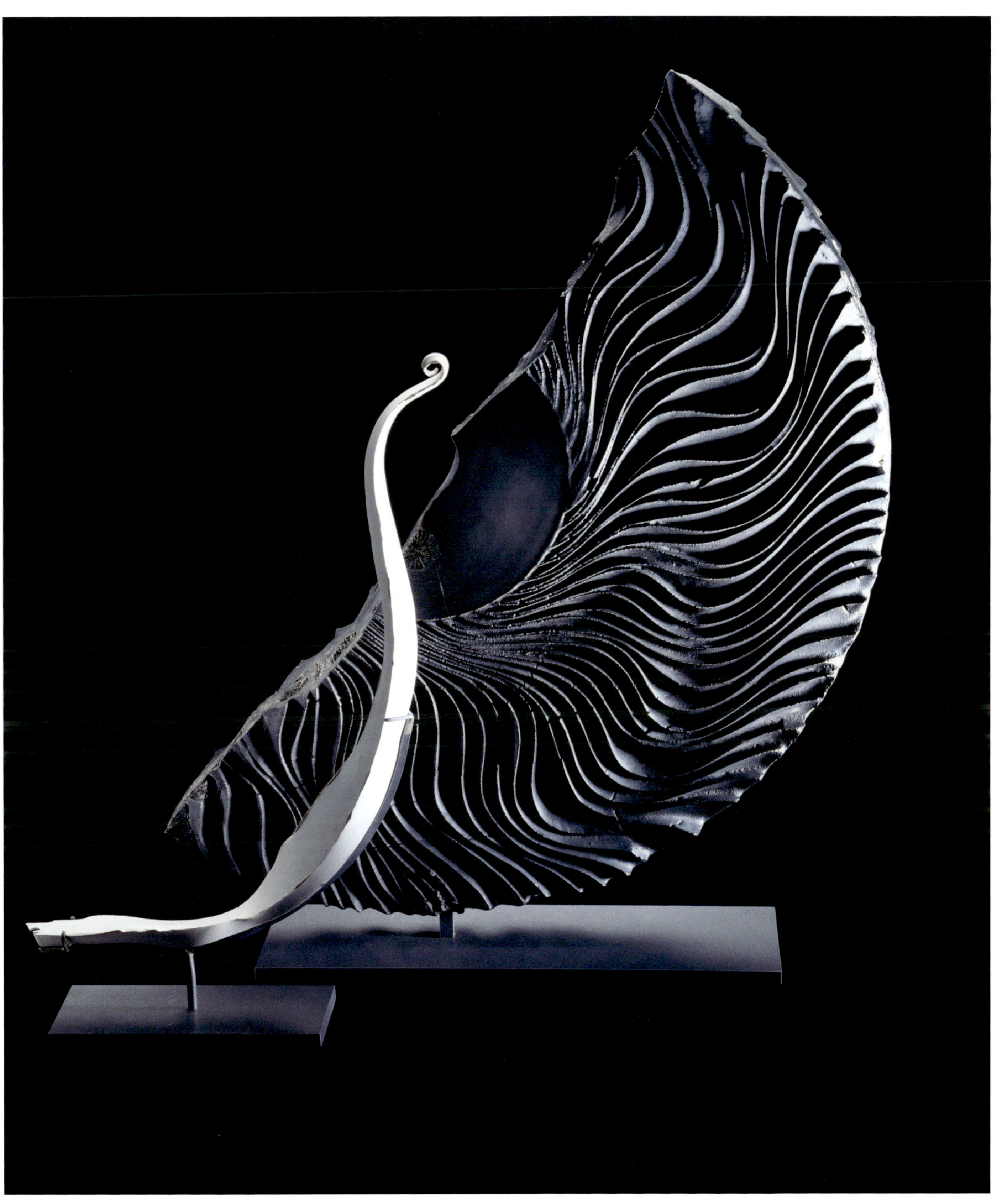

Stone Valley, 2001-02, porcelain, 4 x 4 x 4 in.

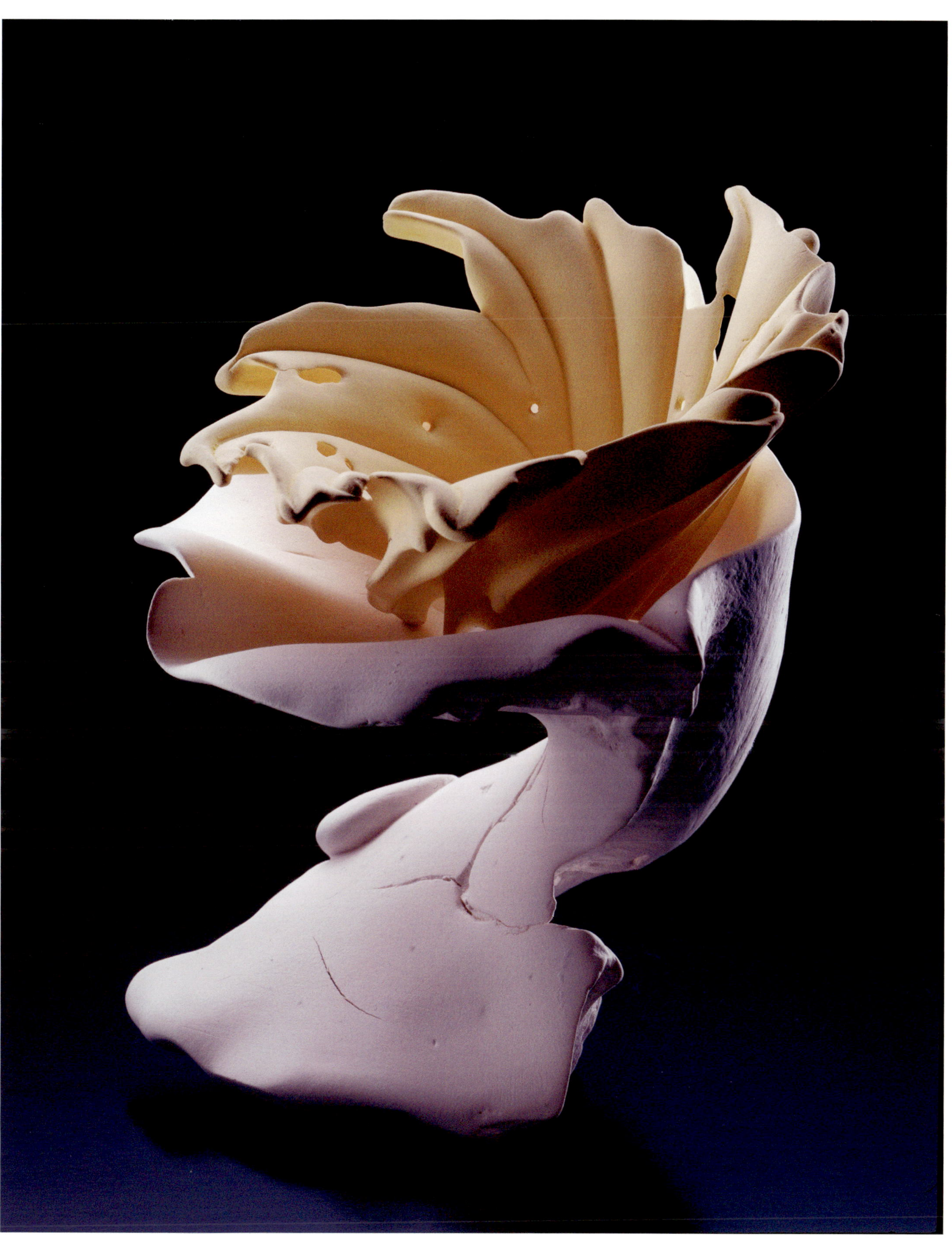

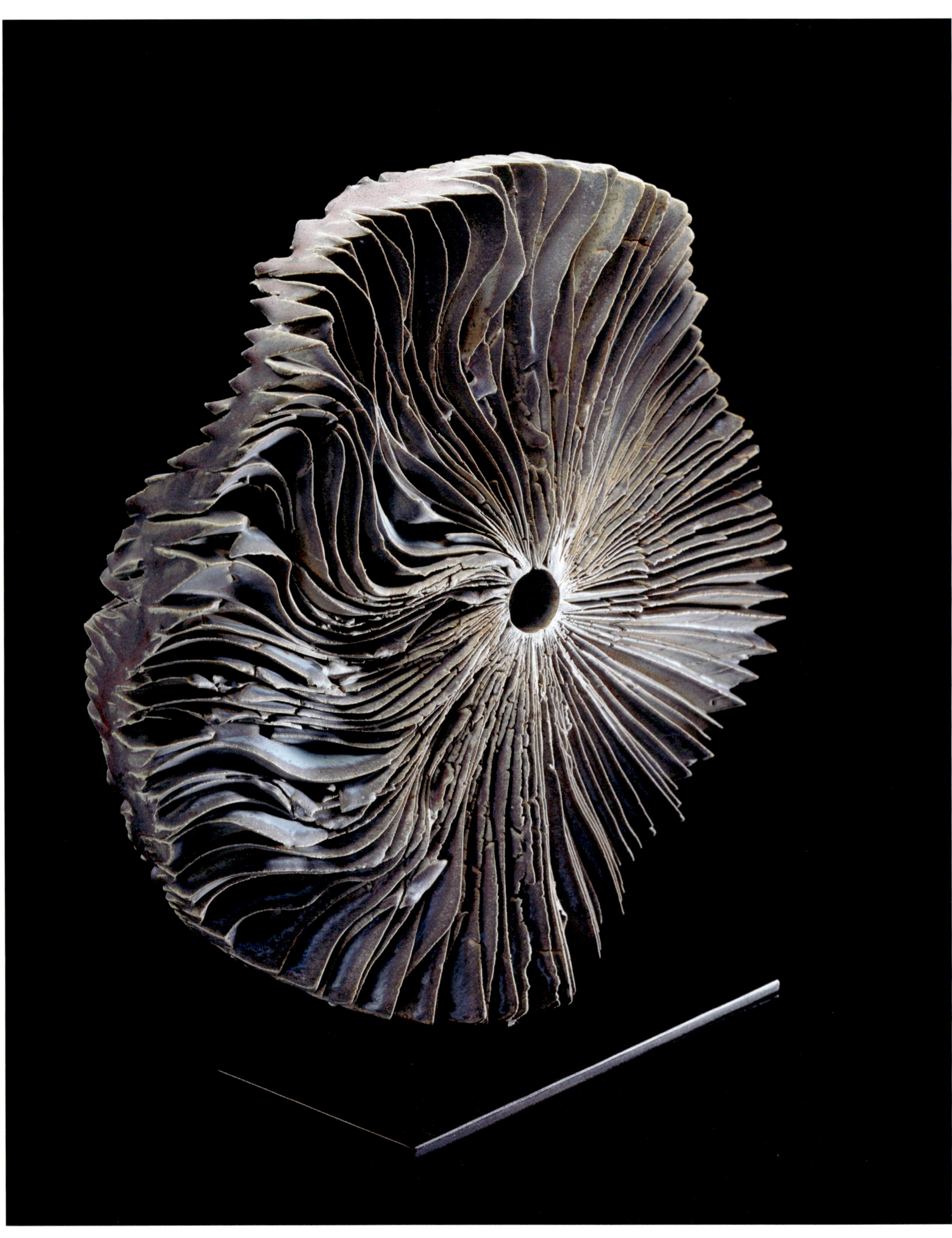

Mauve, side B, 2002-03, glazed stoneware, 17 in. diam. x 4 in.
Collection Daum Museum of Contemporary Art

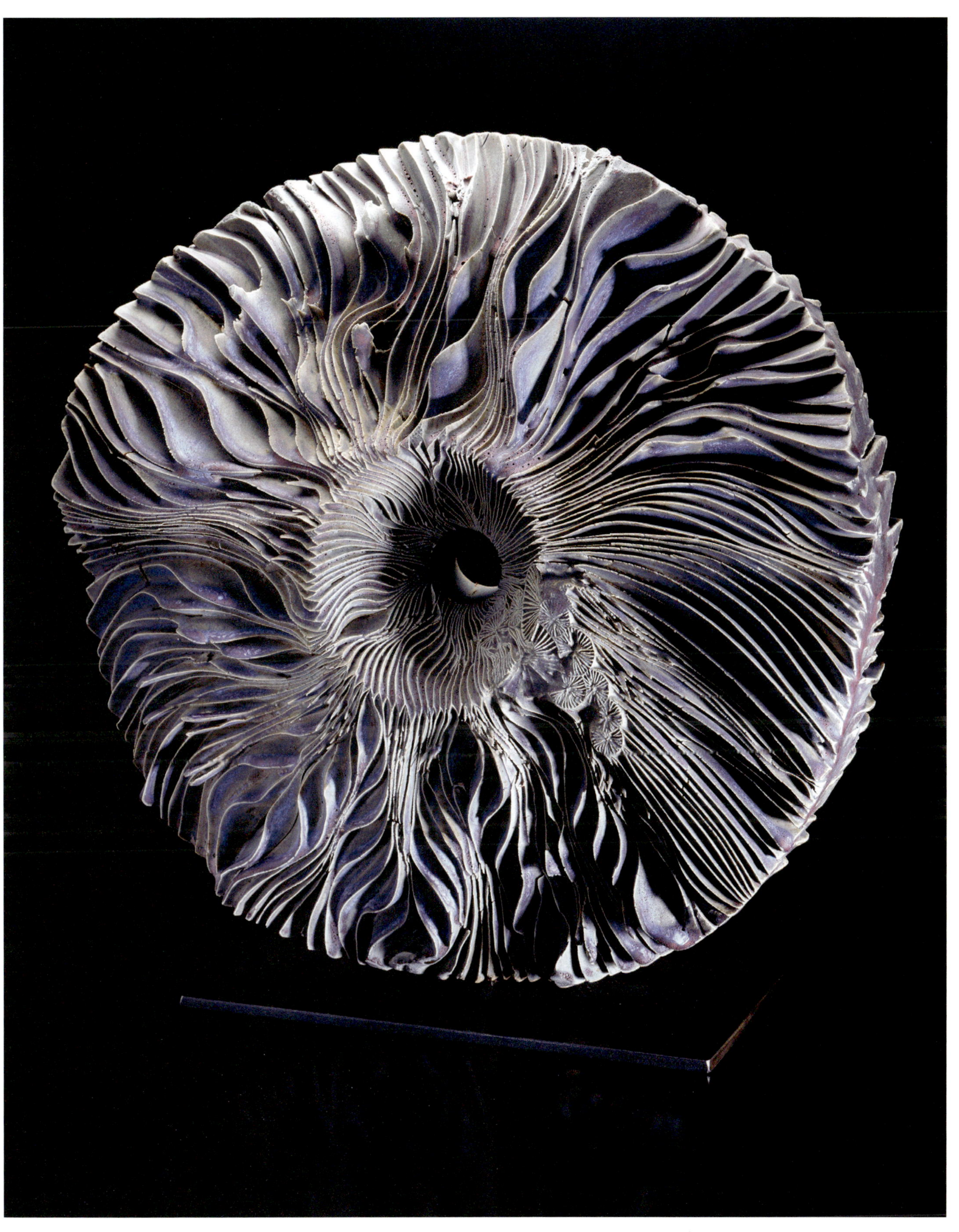

Mauve, side A, 2002-03, glazed stoneware, 17 in. diam. x 4 in.
Collection Daum Museum of Contemporary Art

Hollow Log, 2003, porcelain, 4 x 5 x 4 in.

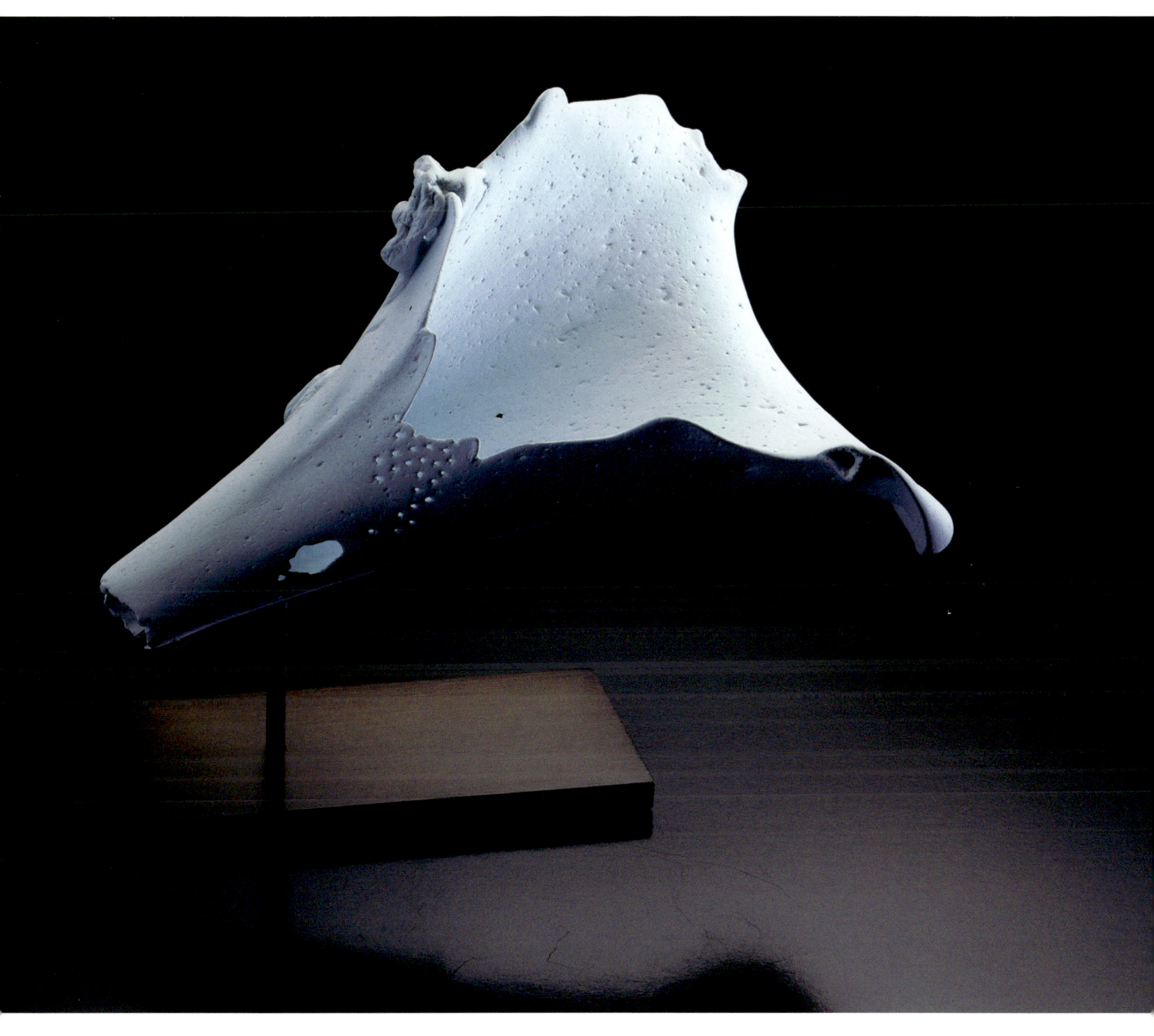

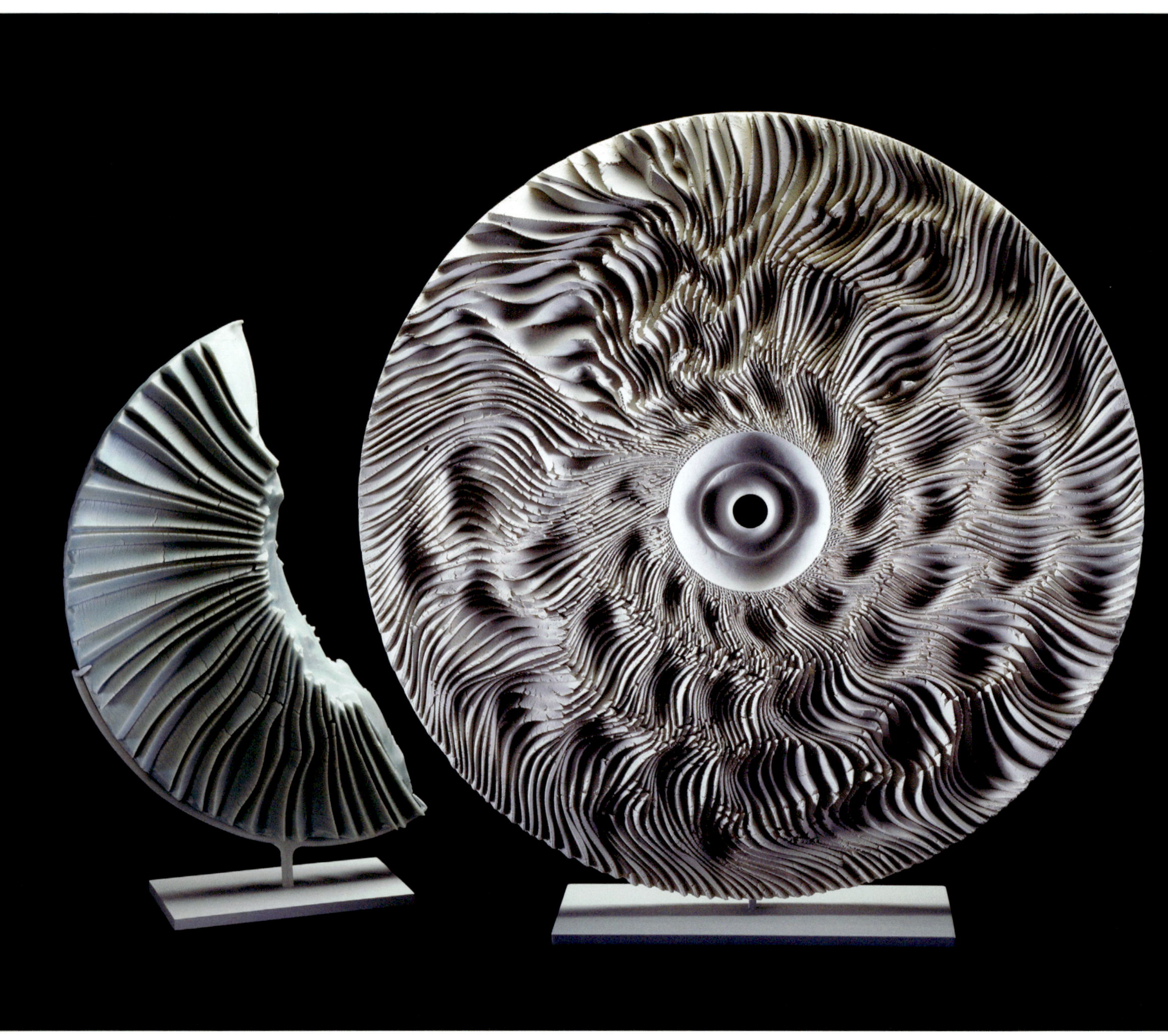

US-Nippon No. 1, side B, 2004, porcelain and glazed porcelain, 19 in. diam. x 2 in.; 12 x 5 x 1 1/2 in.

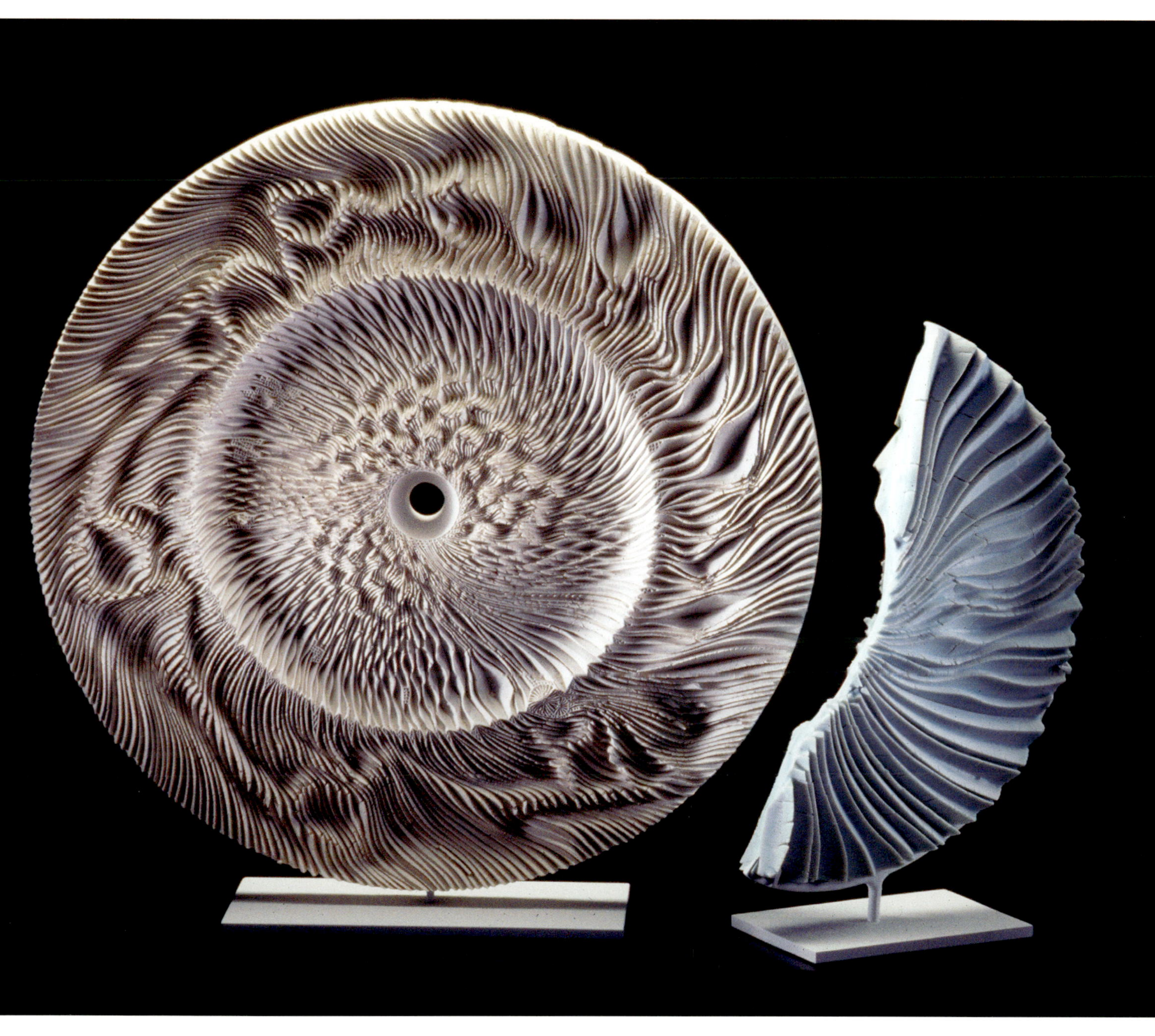

US-Nippon No. 1, side A, 2004, porcelain and glazed porcelain, 19 in. diam. x 2 in.; 12 x 5 x 1 1/2 in.

Emily, 2005, marbled stoneware and porcelain, 7 x 8 x 8 in.

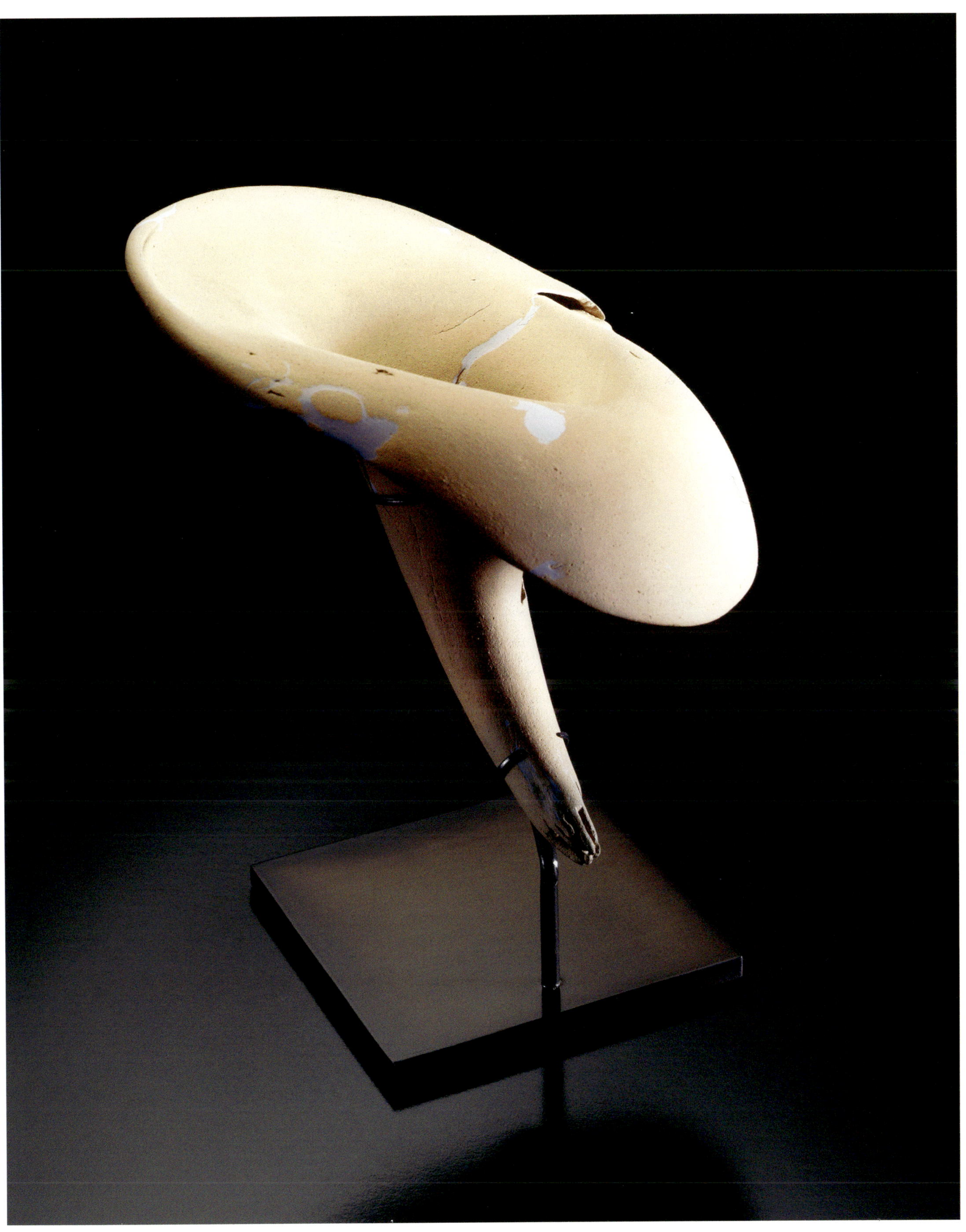

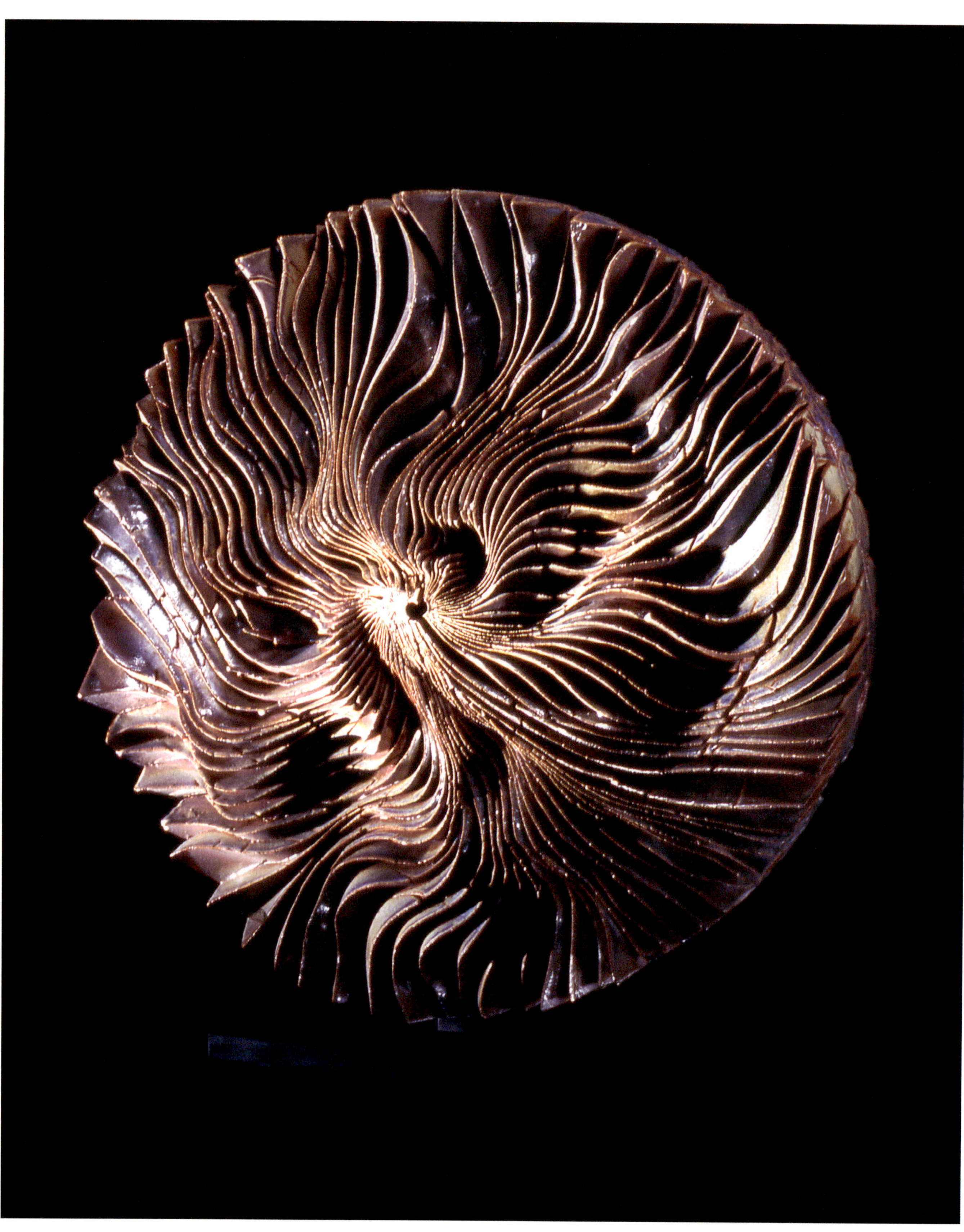

Laocoön, side B, 2006-07, glazed stoneware, 32 in. diam. x 5 in.

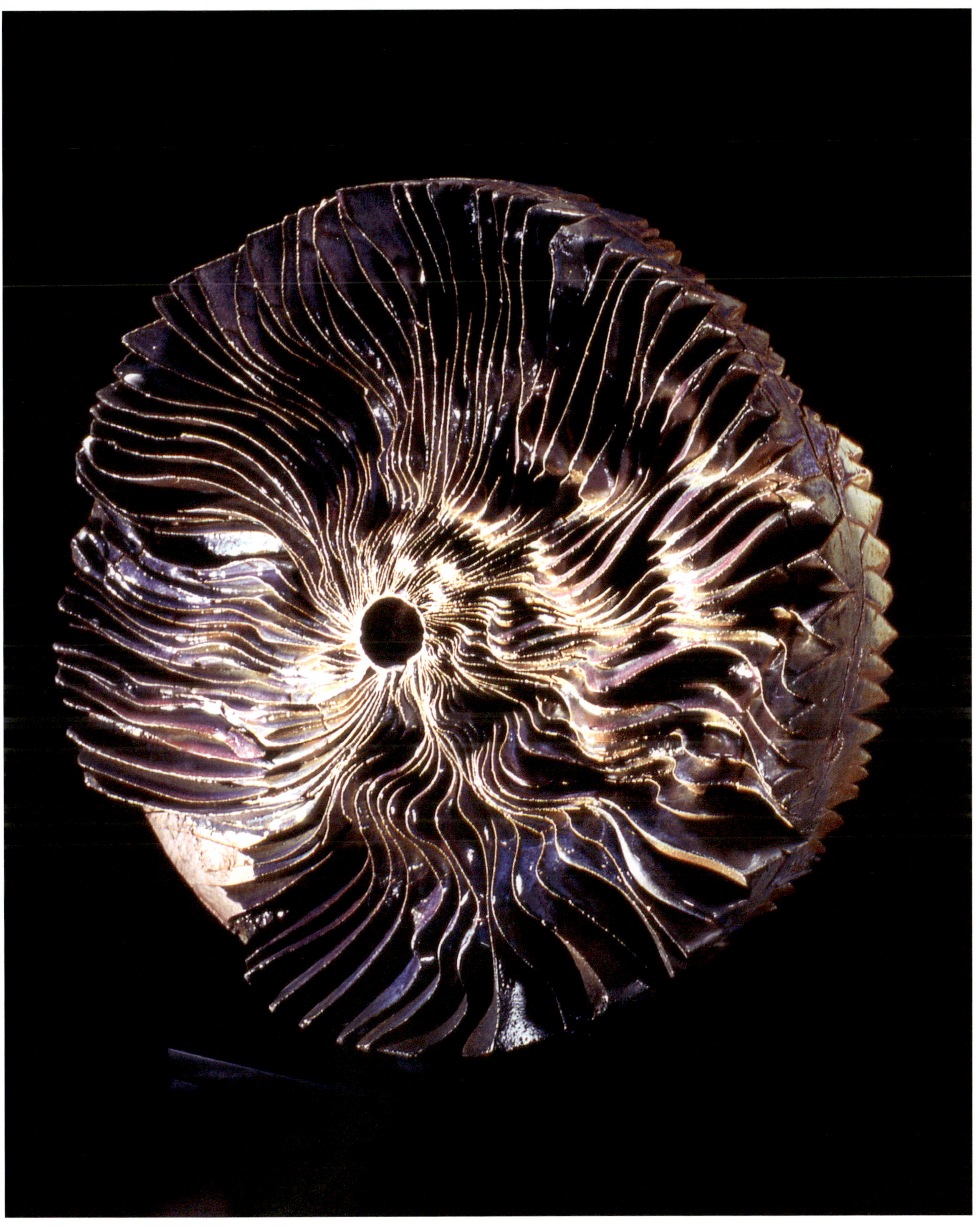

Laocoön, side A, 2006-07, glazed stoneware, 32 in. diam. x 5 in.

Purple, 2008, glazed earthenware, 19 in. diam. x 1 in.

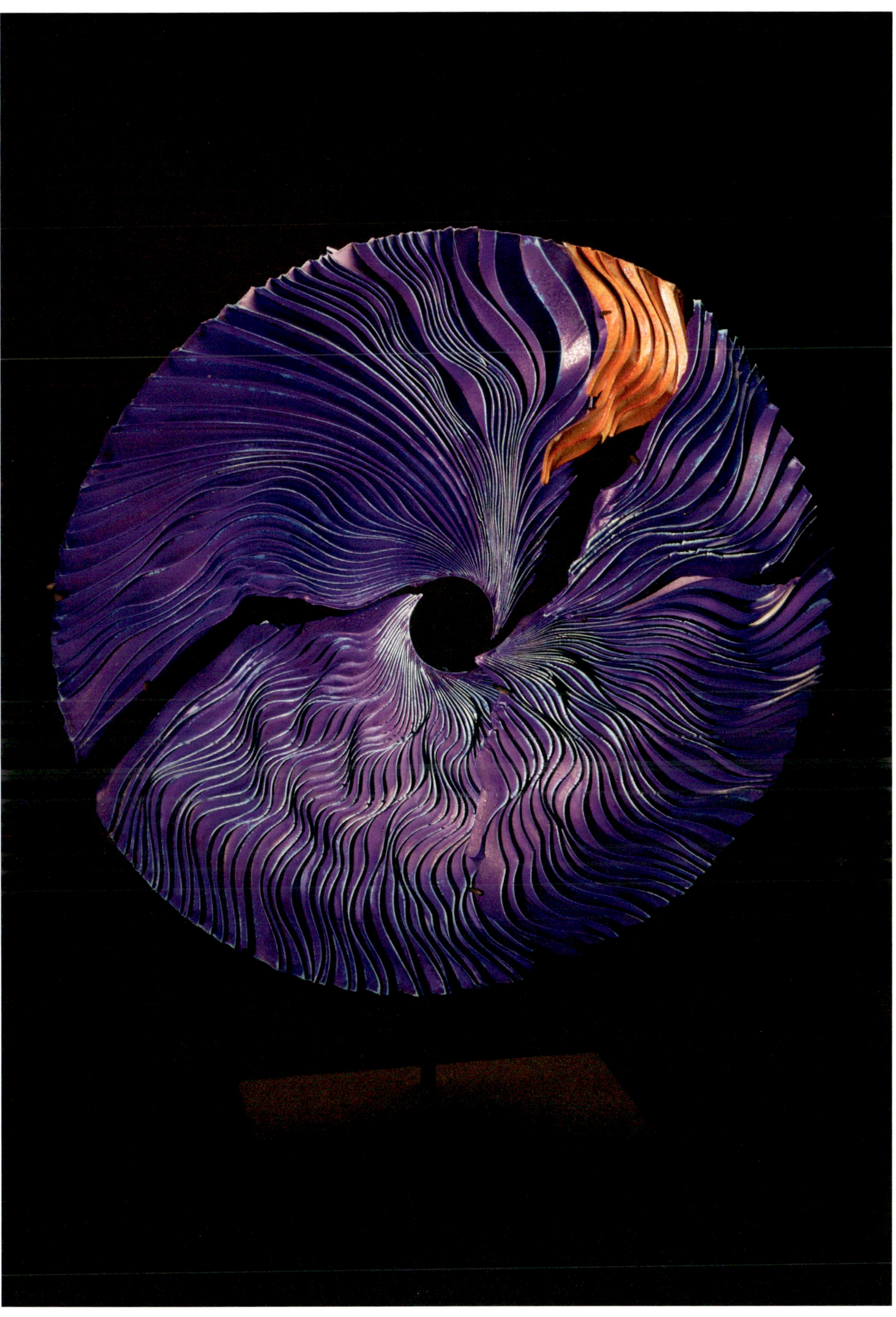

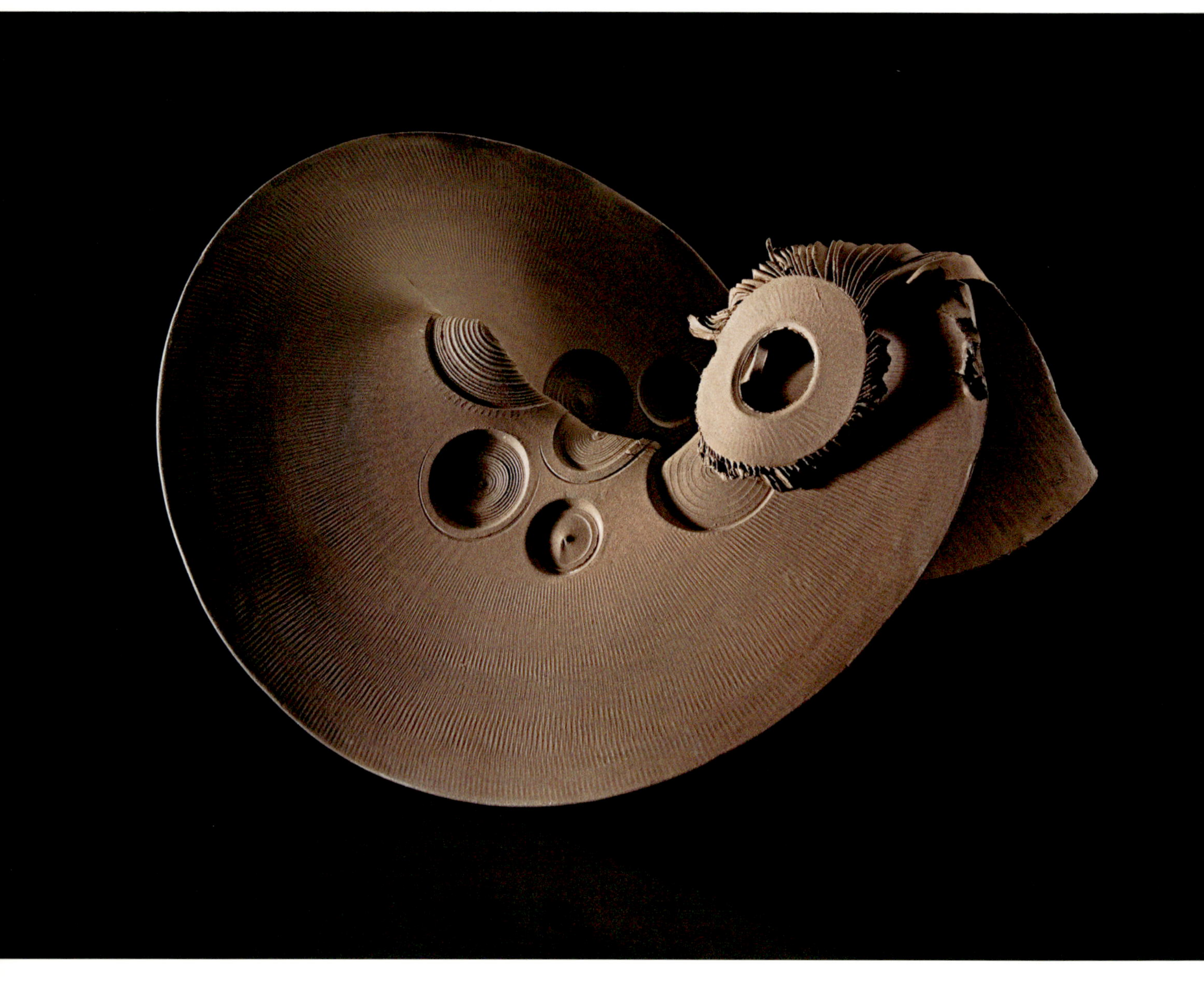

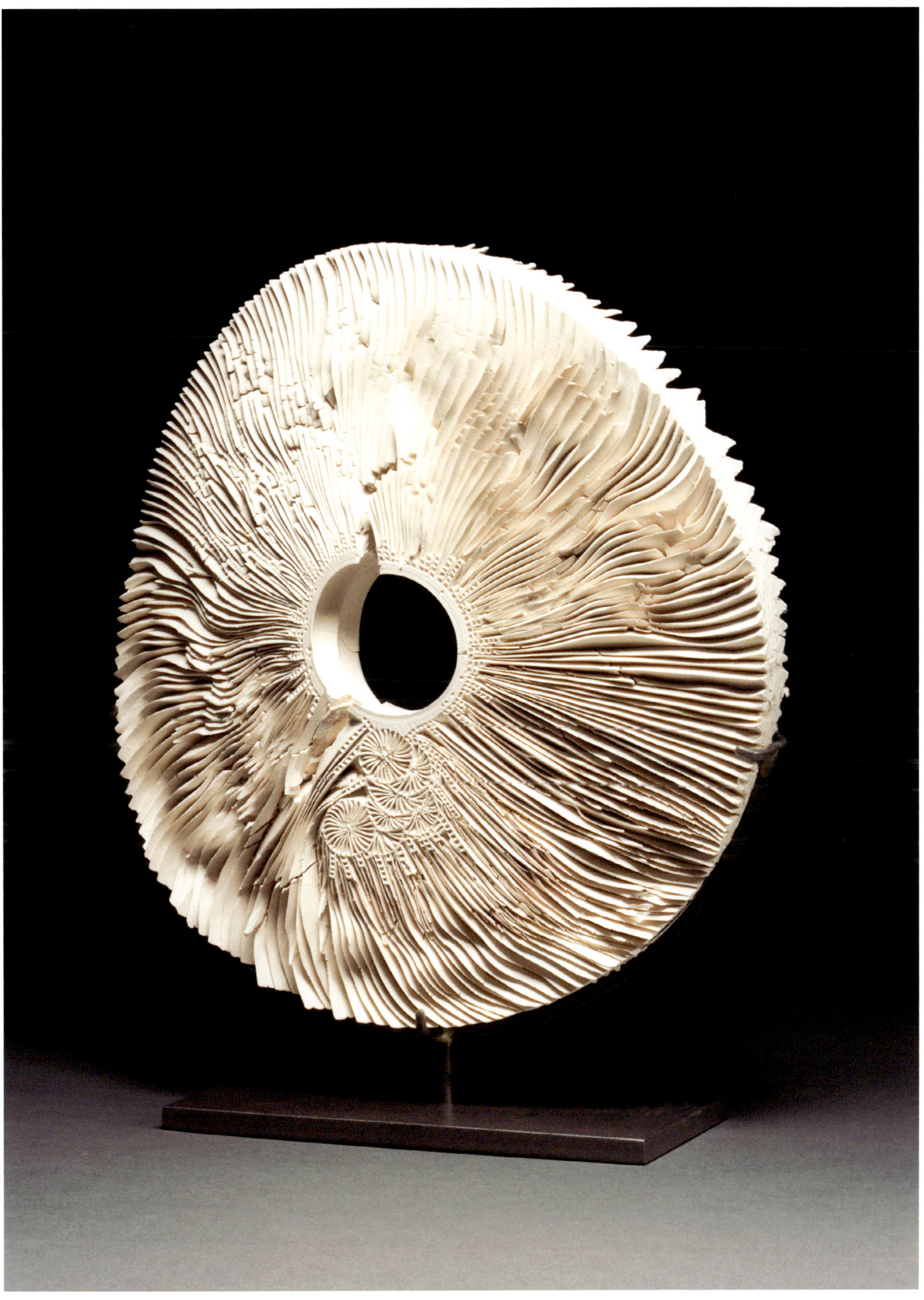

Bent (*Phong's Table*), side B, 2004, porcelain, 8 in. diam. x 2 1/2 in.

Salmancus (*Phong's Table*), 2001-02, porcelain, 9 x 3 x 1/2 in.

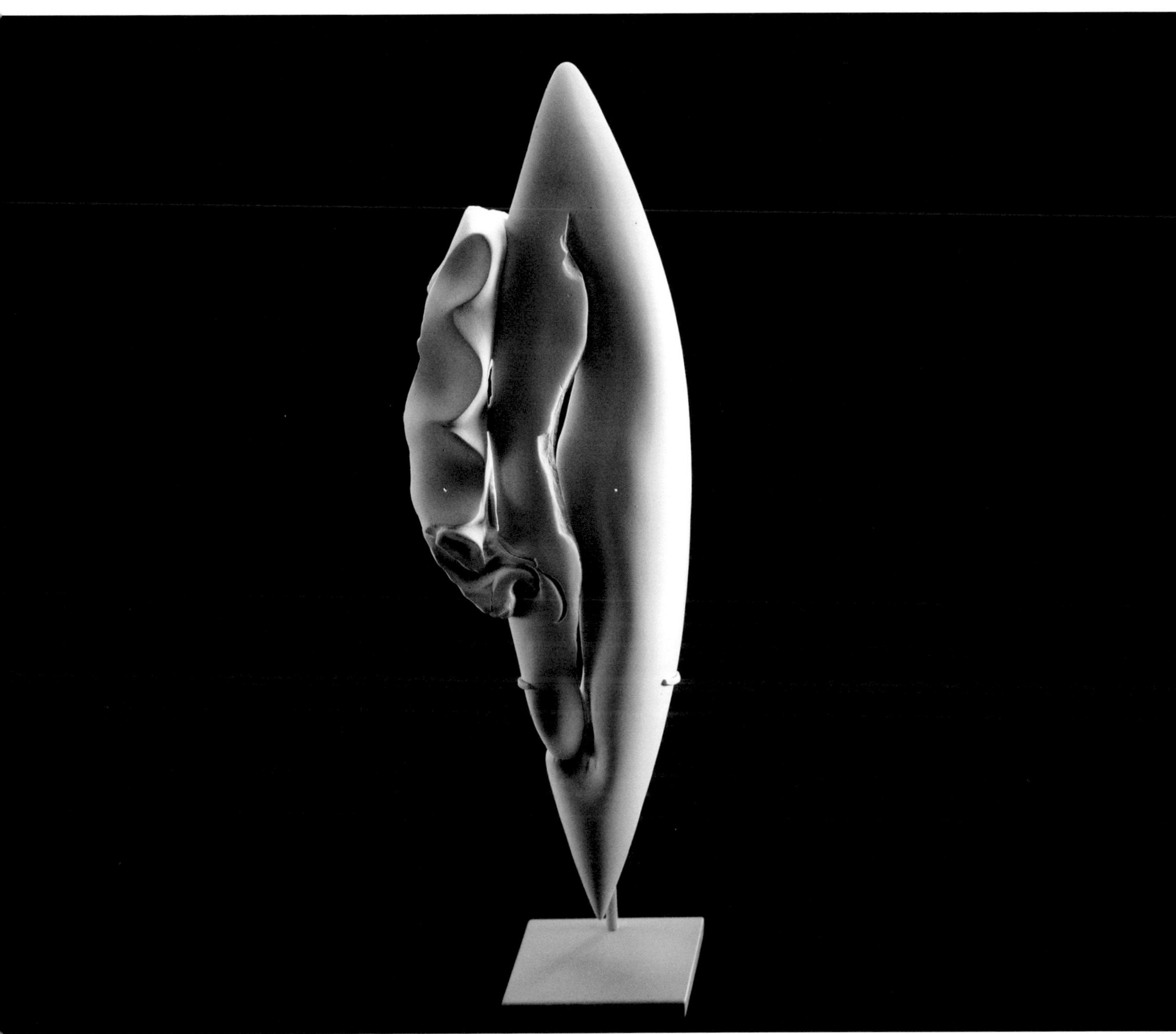

MARC LEUTHOLD

Born in Mount Kisco, New York, 1962

EDUCATION

1988 MFA, University of North Carolina, Chapel Hill, NC

1985 AB, Fine Arts, College of William and Mary, Williamsburg, VA

ACADEMIC APPOINTMENTS

1997-present Professor of Art, State University of New York, Potsdam, NY

2005-06 Visiting Lecturer of Art, Princeton University, Princeton, NJ

2001 Visiting Lecturer of Art, Princeton University, Princeton, NJ

1994-97 Adjunct Professor of Art, Parsons School of Design, New York, NY

SELECTED ARTIST RESIDENCIES

2010 Maison des métiers d'art de Quebec, Quebec City, Canada
Tajimi City, Japan
24th International Symposium of Ceramics, Bechyně, Czech Republic
American Artists Symposium, International Ceramics Studio, Kecskemét, Hungary

2009 Les Ateliers Céramiques de la Fondation Bruckner, Geneva, Switzerland

2008 International Ceramic Studio, Kecskemét, Hungary

2007 FLICAM American Ceramics Art Museum, Fuping, People's Republic of China

2006 Robert M. MacNamara Foundation, Westport Island, ME

2005 Edward F. Albee Foundation, Montauk, NY
I-Park Artists' Enclave, East Haddam, CT
Seto City, Seto, Japan

2003 Seto City, Seto, Japan

2002 I-Park Artists' Enclave, East Haddam, CT

2001 International Ceramic Symposium, Dokuz Eylül University, Izmir, Turkey

1998 New York Experimental Glass Workshop (UrbanGlass), Brooklyn, NY

1997 JINRO International Ceramic Workshop, Kyungnam University, Masan, Republic of Korea

1996 Arts/Industry Residency, John Michael Kohler Arts Center, Sheboygan, WI

1995 Bemis Center for Contemporary Arts, Omaha, NE

1993 The Banff Centre, Banff, Alberta, Canada
La Napoule Art Foundation, La Napoule, France

AWARDS

2008 Rockwell Visiting Artist, The Taft School, Watertown, CT

2003 Special prize, *2nd World Ceramic Biennale,* World Ceramic Exposition Foundation, Icheon, Republic of Korea
Chancellor's Award for Excellence in Research and Creative Activities, State University of New York, Albany, NY

2002 President's Award for Excellence in Research and Creative Endeavors, State University of New York, Potsdam, NY

1999 Elected lifetime member, International Academy of Ceramics, Geneva, Switzerland

COMMISSIONS

2002 *Origin,* Robyn and John Horn, Little Rock, AR

2001-11 LongHouse Medal, LongHouse Reserve, East Hampton, NY

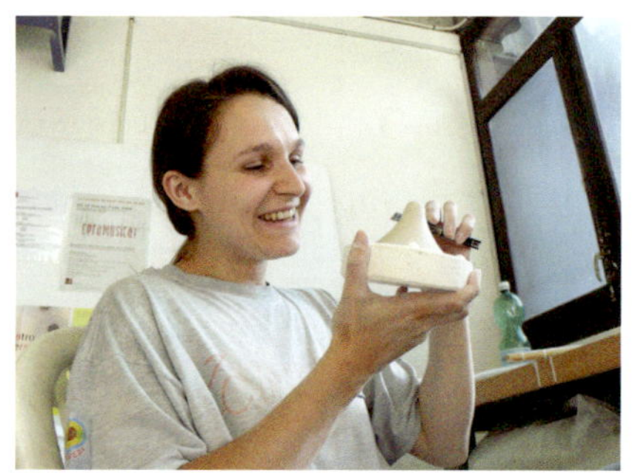

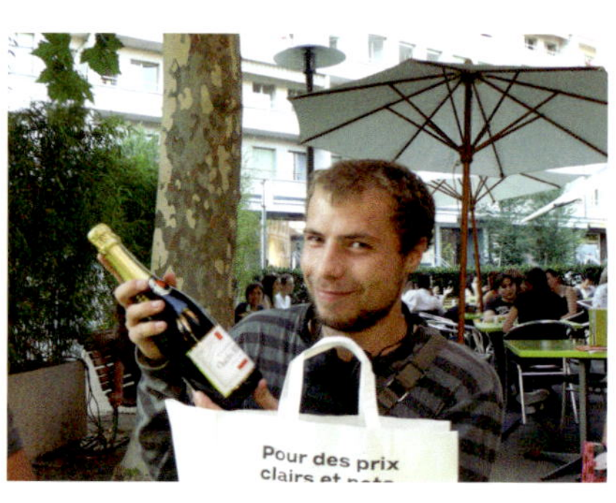

Project assistants Charlyne Kolly and Samuel Gäumann, Les Ateliers Céramiques de la Fondation Bruckner, Geneva, Switzerland, summer 2009.

SELECTED SOLO AND TWO-PERSON EXHIBITIONS

2010 *Marc Leuthold, Sculpture, 1995-2010,* Daum Museum of Contemporary Art, Sedalia, MO

2009 *Faute,* Parcours Céramique, Maya Guidi Gallery, Geneva, Switzerland

2008 *Fault,* Mark Potter Gallery, The Taft School, Watertown, CT

2006 *The Lowest Trees Have Topps,* Pahk International, New York, NY

2004 *Expanding Vortex,* Gallery Pahk, New York, NY (two-person)

2003 *Four Times,* Schein-Joseph International Museum of Ceramic Art, Alfred University, Alfred, NY

2000 *Hints,* Allcott Gallery, Hanes Art Center, Chapel Hill, NC

1999 *Marc Leuthold Ceramics,* Everson Museum of Art, Syracuse, NY

1995 *New Work,* LongHouse Foundation, East Hampton, NY (two-person)

SELECTED GROUP EXHIBITIONS

2009 Art Palm Beach International Art Exposition (Loveed Fine Arts), West Palm Beach, FL

2008 *International Ceramics Biennale,* Yingge Ceramics Museum, New Taipei City, Republic of China
Irrational Profusion, PS1 Contemporary Art Center, Queens, NY
Built: Sculptural Trends in Clay, Osilas Gallery, Concordia University, Bronxville, NY
SOFA New York (Loveed Fine Arts), New York, NY
Art Palm Beach International Art Exposition (Loveed Fine Arts), West Palm Beach, FL

2007 *4th International Ceramics Biennale,* World Ceramic Exposition Foundation, Icheon, Republic of Korea
SOFA New York (Loveed Fine Arts), New York, NY

2006 *World Clay,* Latvian National Museum of Art, Riga, Latvia
Winter Salon, Lesley Heller Gallery, New York, NY
Upstate Visions, Loveed Fine Arts, New York, NY
Two Media/Two Expressions, Springfield Museum of Art, Springfield, OH
SOFA New York (Loveed Fine Arts), New York, NY

2005 SOFA Chicago (Sherrie Gallerie), Chicago, IL
Artists-in-Residence in Seto 2002-5, Seto City Museum, Seto, Japan
SOFA New York (Loveed Fine Arts), New York, NY

2004 *Summer for Some,* Kraushaar Galleries, New York, NY
International Academy of Ceramics Member Exhibit, Icheon World Ceramic Center, Icheon, Republic of Korea
Céramique Contemporaine, Musée Ariana, Geneva, Switzerland
Artists-in-Residence in Seto 2002-5, Gallery 1, Tokyo, Japan
Jack Lenor Larsen: Creator and Collector, Museum of Art & Design, New York, NY
SOFA New York (Loveed Fine Arts), New York, NY

2003 *Clay Works: American Ceramics from the Everson Museum of Art,* UBS PaineWebber Art Gallery, New York, NY
2nd International Ceramics Biennale, World Ceramic Exposition Foundation, Icheon, Republic of Korea
59th Scripps College Invitational, Ruth Chandler Williamson Gallery, Scripps College, Los Angeles, CA
Modern Medium, Fenimore Art Museum, Cooperstown, NY
SOFA New York (Loveed Fine Arts), New York, NY

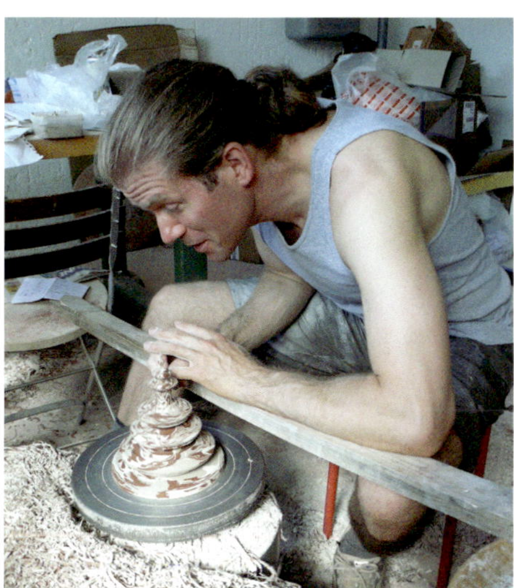

Marc Leuthold at work on a component of *Offering,* Les Ateliers Céramiques de la Fondation Bruckner, Geneva, Switzerland, summer 2009.

2002 Art Palm Beach International Art Exposition (Nancy Hoffman Gallery), West Palm Beach, FL
Objects of Desire, Nancy Hoffman Gallery, New York, NY
International Ceramics Invitational, State Gallery of Fine Arts, Izmir, Turkey
National Ceramics Invitational, Armory Art Center, West Palm Beach, FL
Coming of Age, Mint Museum of Art, Charlotte, NC
USA Clay, Renwick Gallery, Smithsonian American Art Museum, Washington, DC
SOFA New York (Loveed Fine Arts), New York, NY

2000 *6th Taiwan Golden Ceramics Awards,* Yingko Ceramics Museum, Taipei, Republic of China
Living with Form, Horn Collection, Arkansas Art Center, Little Rock, AR
Allan Chasanoff Collection, Mint Museum of Art, Charlotte, NC
Defining Craft 1, American Craft Museum, New York, NY
SOFA New York (Loveed Fine Arts), New York, NY

1999 *Clay into Art: Selections from the Ceramics Collection of the Metropolitan Museum of Art,* Metropolitan Museum of Art, New York, NY

1997 *JINRO International Ceramic Art,* Seoul Art Center, Seoul, Republic of Korea

1995 *Fletcher Challenge Ceramics Award,* Auckland Museum, Auckland, New Zealand

1993 *Talentbörse Handwerk,* Internationale Handwerksmesse, Munich, Germany
Fiction, Function, Figuration: The 29th Ceramic National, Everson Museum of Art, Syracuse, NY

1992 *XIII International Biennial of Ceramic Arts,* Vallauris, France

1991 *Anticipation '91,* Chicago International New Art Forms Expo, Chicago, IL

1990 *Biennial Exhibition,* Mint Museum of Art, Charlotte, NC
Interiors, North Carolina Museum of Art, Raleigh, NC

SELECTED BIBLIOGRAPHY

"Acquisitions." *American Craft,* April-May 1997.

"Antennae." *The World of Interiors,* February 1997.

"Commissions." *American Craft,* December 2002-January 2003.

"Gallery." *American Craft,* August-September 2004.

"Gallery." *American Craft,* October-November 1996.

"Marc Leuthold." *Ceramics Monthly,* November 1995.

"New Faces at Navy Pier." *Ceramics Monthly,* February 1992.

"Portfolio." *American Craft,* June/July 1994.

Bethany, Marilyn. "What Is in Store." *New York Magazine,* February 1991.

Brown, Glen R. "Marc Leuthold's 'Fault': Situating Sculpture." *Ceramics Monthly,* March 2009.

———. "Marc Leuthold: The Infinite Non-Objective." *Ceramics: Art and Perception*, March-May 2006.

Clinger, Julia. "Art School Exhibition." *Chautauquan Daily,* July 23-24, 1994.

Cushing, Val. *The Ceramic Design Book: A Gallery of Contemporary Work*, 156. New York: Lark Books, 1998.

Cutajar, Mario. "Marc Leuthold's Good Form." In *Marc Leuthold, Ceramics,* np. Syracuse, NY: Everson Museum of Art, 1999.

———. "A Nostalgia for Beauty." *Art Week Magazine,* September 1995.

———. "LongHouse Exhibition Review." *American Ceramics* 12, no. 1 (1995).

Fairbanks, Jonathan, and Angela Fina. *The Best of Pottery*, 39. Gloucester, MA: Rockport Publishers, Inc., 1996.

Giuduci, Nicolas, and Germaine Varnier. "Une vue imprenable sur l'art contemporain." *Nice Matin*, November 15, 1993.

Hopper, Robin. *Making Marks: Discovering the Ceramic Surface*, 67, 128. Iola, WI: Krause Publications, 2004.

Lane, Peter. *Contemporary Studio Porcelain,* cover, 2, 84, 106-8, 176, 247. 2nd ed. Philadelphia: University of Pennsylvania Press, 2003.

Larsen, Jack Lenor. "Reflections on Contemporary Design." In *Fiberarts Design Book Five*, 9. Ashville, NC: Lark Books, 1995.

Lauria, Jo. "Scripps Annual: Clay and the Nature of Things." *Ceramics: Art and Perception,* March 2003.

Leuthold, Marc. "Making Art in Hungary." *New Ceramics,* April 2009.

———. "Marc Leuthold's New Forms." *The NCECA Journal* 26 (March 2005): 23-24.

———. "Emerging Artists: Marc Leuthold." *The NCECA Journal* 18 (March 1997): 105-6.

Leuthold, Marc, with Sarah G. Wilkins. "From Average to Excellent." *Ceramics Monthly*, March 2008.

———. "Lessons from a City Kiln." In *Studio Practices, Techniques and Tips: A Collection of Articles from Ceramics Monthly*, edited by Anderson Turner, 119-21. Westerville, OH: American Ceramic Society, 2004.

Levin, Elaine. "Eco Rhythmics: Color and Texture in Clay." *Kerameiki Techni*, December 2002.

Merino, Tony. "29th US Clay National." *Ceramics: Art and Perception,* issue 14, 1994.

Ming, Bai. *World-famous Ceramic Artists' Studios*, 214-29. Beijing: Hebei Fine Arts Publishing House, 2005.

Perreault, John. "Marc Leuthold."*American Craft,* December 2006-January 2007.

———. "The Center Holds." In *Marc Leuthold: The Center Holds,* 10-13. Westerville, OH: American Ceramic Society, 2003.

———. "Marc Leuthold: The Center Holds." *Kerameiki Techni,* April 2003.

———. "Big Apple Clay. Is There a New York School of Ceramics? 'Marc Leuthold.'" *American Ceramics* 14, no. 2 (2003): 26-27.

Peterson, Susan. *The Craft and Art of Clay*, 62, 87. London: Laurence King Publishing Ltd., 2003.

———. *Contemporary Ceramics*, 50. New York: Watson-Guptill, 2000.

Peterson, Susan, and Jan Peterson. *Working with Clay*, 101. London: Laurence King Publishing Ltd., 2002.

Piché Jr., Thomas. "Marc Leuthold—Cosmographies." In *Marc Leuthold, Ceramics,* np. Syracuse, NY: Everson Museum of Art, 1999.

———. "Clay Works: American Ceramics from the Collection of the Everson Museum of Art." *Kerameiki Techni,* April 2003.

Reichert, Elizabeth. "Built: Sculptural Trends in Clay." *Ceramics Monthly,* February 2009.

Sansegundo, Sheridan. "At the Galleries." *The East Hampton Star*, May 4, 1995.

Schein-Joseph International Museum of Ceramic Art. "Four Times: An Installation by Marc Leuthold." *Ceramophile,* fall 2002.

Shiverdecker, Adam, ed. "Marc Leuthold." *Panhandler: Contemporary Ceramic Artists Issue* (fall 2010): 46-53.

Trieschmann, Werner. "Collecting a Life: John & Robyn Horn." *American Craft,* December 2000-January 2001.

Vivas, Antonio. "Mark (sic) Leuthold." *Revista Cerámica,* no. 96 (2005).

Williams, Gerry. "Open Hands, International Academy of Ceramics." *The Studio Potter,* December 2002.

Wilkins, Sarah G. "Marc Leuthold." *Ceramics Monthly,* June-August 2002.

———. "Marc Leuthold: The Evolution of the Wheel." *Neue Keramik,* January-February 2002.

Yelle, Richard Wilfred. *Glass Art from UrbanGlass*, 136. Atglen, PA: Schiffer Publishing, 2000.

Zakin, Richard. *Ceramics: Mastering the Craft*, 104. Iola, WI: Krause Publications, 2001.

SELECTED PUBLIC COLLECTIONS

Arkansas Arts Center, Little Rock, AR

Benaki Museum, Athens, Greece

Bemis Center for Contemporary Arts, Omaha, NE

Brooklyn Museum, Brooklyn, NY

Daum Museum of Contemporary Art, Sedalia, MO

Dokuz Eylül University, Izmir, Turkey

Everson Museum of Art, Syracuse, NY

FuLe International Ceramic Museums, Fuping, People's Republic of China

Icheon World Ceramic Center, Icheon, Republic of Korea

John Michael Kohler Arts Center, Sheboygan, WI

Latvian National Museum of Art, Riga, Latvia

LongHouse Reserve, East Hampton, NY

Metropolitan Museum of Art, New York, NY

Mint Museum of Art, Charlotte, NC

Musée Ariana, Geneva, Switzerland

Museum of Art & Design, New York, NY

Museum of Fine Arts, Boston, MA

Museum of Fine Arts, Houston, TX

National Museum of Ceramics in Sèvres, Sèvres, France

Renwick Gallery, Smithsonian American Art Museum, Washington, DC

Seto City Cultural Center, Seto City, Japan

UrbanGlass, Brooklyn, NY

Yingge Ceramics Museum, New Taipei City, Republic of China

CHECKLIST OF THE EXHIBITION

All works courtesy of the artist, unless otherwise noted.

Banff, 1993
glazed stoneware, 11 x 16 x ½ in.

Bronze Hemisphere, 1994
glazed stoneware, 7 x 14½ in. diam.

Ellipse, 1995
glazed porcelain, 8½ x 15 x 3 in.

Westerwald Hemisphere, 1999
wood-fired stoneware, 7½ x 11 in. diam.

Boehme (Red), 1998-99
glazed earthenware, 17 in. diam. x 2 in.

Demi, 2001-04; 2 parts:
a. glazed stoneware, 15 x 9 x 2 in.
b. unglazed stoneware, 9 x 7 x ½ in.

Stone Valley, 2001-02
porcelain, 4 x 4 x 4 in.

Mauve, 2002-03
glazed stoneware, 17 in. diam. x 4 in.
Collection of Daum Museum of Contemporary Art

Hollow Log, 2003
porcelain, 4 x 5 x 4 in.

Brain, 2004
glazed porcelain, 5 x 6 x 4 in.

US-Nippon No. 1, 2004; 2 parts:
a. porcelain, 19 in. diam. x 2 in.
b. glazed porcelain, 12 x 5 x 1½ in.

Emily, 2005
marbled stoneware and porcelain, 7 x 8 x 8 in.

Storm, 2005-06
glazed stoneware, 17 x 10 x 5 in.

Fish, 2005-06
glazed and unglazed porcelain, 3 parts:
a. 4 x 6 x 5 in.
b. 1 x 4 x 3 in.
c. 2 x 3 x 4 in.

Laocoön, 2006-07
glazed stoneware, 22 in. diam. x 5 in.

Lotus, 2006-08
glazed porcelain, 36 in. diam. x 2 in.

Purple, 2008
glazed earthenware, 19 in. diam. x 1 in.

Danaë, 2008-09
glazed earthenware, 14 in. diam. x ½ in.

Bent (Phong's Table), 2004
porcelain, 8 in. diam. x 2½ in.

Rococo (Phong's Table), 2002
porcelain, 12 in. diam. x 2 in.

Hemisphere (Phong's Table), 2005
porcelain, 16 in. diam. x 7 in.

Attic Red Spool with Graffiti (Phong's Table), 2003;
2 parts:
a. earthenware, 7 in. diam. x 1 in.
b. synthetic polymer, 2 x 6 x 1 in.

Salmancus (Phong's Table), 2001-02
porcelain, 9 x 3 x ½ in.

Hermaphroditos (Receptor) (Phong's Table), 2006
porcelain, 6 x 7 x 6 in.

Maureen (Receptor) (Phong's Table), 2006
marbled porcelain and stoneware, 4 x 6 x 4 in.

Black Receptor (Phong's Table), 2002
porcelain, 3 x 3 x 3 in.

Ismir (Phong's Table), 2001
porcelain, 3 x 3 x 3 in.

Cone (Phong's Table), 2006
marbled porcelain and stoneware, 5 in. diam. x 4 in.

Ugly (Phong's Table), 2006
porcelain, 5 in. diam. x 5 in.

Flight, 2009
stoneware, 9 x 10½ x 6¼ in.
Collection of John and Robyn Horn

Pillow, 2009
stoneware, 4 x 8¾ x 3¾ in.
Collection of John and Robyn Horn

Wave, 2009
stoneware, 5 x 9¼ x 6 in.
Collection of John and Robyn Horn

Offering (installation), 2009
porcelain and stoneware, dimensions variable